Offsides!

5515-HENR

Offsides!

Fred Wyant's Provocative Look Inside the National Football League

Rene A. Henry

5515-HENR

Other Books by
Rene A. Henry

How to Profitably Buy and Sell Land

Marketing Public Relations–the hows that make it work!

*You'd Better Have a Hose If You Want to Put Out the Fire–
the complete guide to crisis and risk communications*

*MIUS and you–the builder looks at a new utility concept
(co-authored with Joseph Honick, Richard O'Neill and Fernando Oaxaca)*

*Bears Handbook–stories, stats and stuff about Baylor University football
(co-authored with Mike Bishop)*

Library of Congress Number: 2001116853
ISBN #:   Hardcover   0-7388-7895-2
                     Softcover   0-7388-0973-X

Library of Congress Cataloging-in-Publication Data:

Henry, Rene A., 1933-

        Offsides! Fred Wyant's provocative look inside the NFL / Rene A.
Henry – 1st ed.

p.   cm.

Includes bibliographical references and index.

1. Sports 2. Football. 3. Professional football. 4. National Football
League 5. Officiating. 6. Biography. I. Title

First Edition, 2001
10 9 8 7 6 5 4 3 2 1

This book was printed in the United States of America.

To order additional copies of this book, contact:
Xlibris Corporation
1-888-795-4274
www.Xlibris.com
Orders@Xlibris.com

5515-HENR

For help in making this book possible, the author wishes to give special thanks to Don Smith, Orlando, Fla.; Jerry Bergman, Pittsburgh, Pa.; Greg Aiello, NFL; Art McNally, Philadelphia, Pa.; Greg Bensel, New Orleans Saints; Harvey Greene, Miami Dolphins; Ron Wahl, Pittsburgh Steelers; Matt Marini, NFL Properties; L. Budd Thalman, Penn State University; John Mosher, Arlington, Va.; Sam Huff, Middleburg, Va.; and all of those interviewed who generously gave of their time.

Cover Photograph
The cover photograph of the legendary Vince Lombardi expressing his feelings to Fred Wyant was taken by Wally McNamee. It was one of the prize winning photographs in the annual White House News Photographers Association competition.

Author Photograph
Photograph of the author on the back cover by Jeffery M. Alper

Contents

FOREWORD

Never before have players, coaches, team owners, the media and fans been as angry, critical and outspoken of sports officiating as they have been in recent years. This is happening in professional football, basketball and baseball and even in intercollegiate sports. As the complaints have increased, so have the fines assessed by commissioners of the NFL, NBA and Major League Baseball. I am told that one professional basketball coach was so outraged by the officiating that following the game he retired in mid-season.

The referees, umpires and officials responsible for overseeing the conduct of the game are human. Humans make mistakes. Even computers and machines make mistakes, as we learned about the voting machines in Florida during the 2000 presidential election.

Thanks to modern sports medicine, players in all sports are bigger, stronger, quicker and faster than ever before. And, while there are more officials on the field of play today than there were 20 years ago, action happens faster than the human eye can see.

Instant replay is not perfect, but in most cases it is better than no replay at all. Television often does not have all of the camera angles needed to make the right call. When game action is replayed on jumbo screens in the stadium, it only serves to provoke and anger the fans, especially if the call is against the home team.

During the 2000 season, NFL officials apologized to the Pittsburgh Steelers after officials made wrong calls in three different games. The Steelers lost all three games, two of them by only three points, and one in overtime. A correct call in just one of the three games could have put the Steelers in the post-season playoffs. Now even college coaches are asking for a similar replay system. Conference commissioners agree mistakes are made, but caution against a replay system because of logistical problems in equipping the stadiums.

So much of officiating is judgment. Judgment comes from experience and maturity. Veteran officials mentor, train and coach rookie and younger officials. When senior leadership is not available in a league, it does affect the quality of the officiating. In 1998, the National Basketball Association lost several of its veteran referees who pleaded guilty to federal income tax evasion. The league was concerned about losing as many as 15 of its team of 58 for the same reason. The referees downgraded first-class airline tickets to coach and did not report the difference as income. Some were eventually reinstated, but one has to question the ethics and integrity of such action. Major League Baseball had virtually no turnover until many of its umpires went on strike and lost their jobs.

When Jerry Seeman replaced Art McNally in 1990 as director of officiating, the NFL began losing many of its best officials. From 1991 to 1997, the league lost 54 of 112 officials–many not by their choice. No *Fortune 500* company could survive losing 48% of its senior management during a comparable period of time. Those in the know say that it takes five years to become a competent, professional NFL official. In 1998, nine senior officials retired with a combined 177 years of experience. In 1990, McNally had 16 officials with 20 or more years of experience compared to only nine for Seeman in 1998. There is no replacement for experience. With the turnover, the league lost a generation of outstanding officials.

NFL officials have been plagued other problems. During a December 19, 1999 game, referee Jeff Triplette threw his yellow penalty flag and it accidentally hit Cleveland lineman Orlando Brown in the eye. Brown, whose father is blind from glaucoma, and concerned about his own eyesight, was outraged and pushed Triplette to the ground. He had just signed a six-year, $27 million contract that included a $7.5 million signing bonus and was professional football's highest paid offensive lineman. Brown, who was hospitalized for six days, was suspended for the last two games. He was reinstated in February, but his contract terminated in August when he was physically unable to train with the Browns. He now is suing the NFL.

To prevent any future injury to players, the league redesigned its yellow penalty flags. Officials used to weight a corner of their flags with various items that included shotgun and BB pellets, fishing weights, popcorn kernels and pennies. The standardized flags are now weighted with sand.

When officials really blunder they become monologue material for Jay Leno and David Letterman. Remember the coin toss controversy? Sitcom writers also take their shots. One did with the dialog for Arliss Michaels, a super pro sports agent, in HBO's television series *Arli$$*, when he said, referring to the credibility of a source for a journalist: "He's about as reliable as an NFL official."

Television announcers too often mislead the public. Many call all officials "referees" when you clearly see the "U" or "HL" on the back of the official's shirt. After reading Chapter II of this book you will know which official is responsible for a call when you see a flag thrown. In one televised game, twice the announcer said: "Let's go to Los Angeles and take a look at the Raider's game." Didn't anyone tell him they are now back in Oakland?

I also question ABC's *Monday Night Football* team as critics of the game. The 2000 season had the lowest ratings in the network's 31-year history. You wonder if they would not be better off on *Saturday Night Live* as the "Not Ready for Primetime Players." The knowledge, insights, humor and even sarcasm of Howard Cosell, Frank Gifford, Alex Karras and Don Meredith are indeed missed.

Being an official in any sport, at any level, is a thankless job. It means absolute dedication and love of the sport. That is why I approached Fred Wyant to give us an inside look at the way it is in the NFL. I always wondered why Fred never was given a Super Bowl assignment. After getting him to open up to me, I now understand why. His peers considered him one of the very best. His mistake was always being outside the system and not playing the game the way his bosses on

Park Avenue expected. When he left the NFL after 27 years, no other official had been in the league as long that had not officiated at least one Super Bowl.

I first met Fred in August 1954. He was the starting quarterback for the West Virginia University Mountaineers football team and had just led the team to a championship season and the Sugar Bowl. I just graduated from The College of William & Mary and was in my first job, as sports information director at WVU. Fred and his teammates gave me a lot to write about during the next two years.

We have been good friends for all these years. I followed his career as an NFL referee and wanted to do this project as a television documentary in the 1970s, but could not get either permission or cooperation from the league. In this book, Fred tells it like it is without any fear of reprisal by the league–why officials make mistakes, the pros and cons of instant replay, the pressure television has put on officiating, the outspoken critics of the game and the greed of new owners who allow players who perform on the field to abuse women, drugs and alcohol off the field.

In the early chapters, the average reader may believe that Fred and his supervisor of officials, Art McNally, were adversaries. However, during a lengthy interview, Art gave me all the time I wanted to ask questions and give his responses. In fact, while Fred and Art may disagree, they do agree to disagree and are friends.

I thank Fred's many NFL colleagues and others who took the time to give me their thoughts on professional football.

This book also may be a first for professional sports. At Fred's request, all profanity has been deleted. This book is G-rated.

On the following pages are Fred Wyant's words and a provocative inside look at the NFL.

–Rene A. Henry
June 2001

This book is dedicated to the coaches and players of the
1952, 1953, 1954 and 1955
West Virginia University football teams –
the greatest football teams in Mountaineer history!

5515-HENR

CHAPTER I

Outside the System

Peeople often ask me how many times I refereed the Super Bowl. They are surprised when I tell them I never worked a Super Bowl. Then they ask: "Well, weren't you an official in the NFL for a long time?" When I tell them, "Yes, I was for 27 years," shocked and surprised, they then ask me: "How in the world could you be a league official for 27 years and never work a Super Bowl?"

To understand why, you need to understand me, my philosophy and the things I believe that are important in life. If I wanted a Super Bowl ring I would have had to be part of the league's system and to play the game the way they wanted it played. To do that would have meant compromising my personal values. Frankly, being happy was much more important.

I became an NFL official in 1966, starting as a line judge. The referee is the team leader and boss on the field. He is in charge of all of the other officials. As a rookie, I was assigned to Art McNally's crew. He was the referee and had been in the league since 1958. He was a perfectionist. He was serious all the time and wanted every official on his crew to be equally as serious. This was a difficult adjustment for me. I was an official in the NFL because I wanted to be there, I liked what I was doing, and wanted to enjoy it. However, I wasn't about to change my lifestyle or personality because someone believed that each and every NFL football game is a life shattering experience. My financial livelihood wasn't dependent on the income I received as an official so it didn't matter whether or not I officiated a professional football game.

The number one key to success is happiness.–Fred Wyant

There was tension between Art McNally and me from day one. My first experience working with him was a pre-season football game. There was a tradition in the league that the rookie on the crew always did the grunt work such as carrying the movie projector and other heavy items, running errands, or doing insignificant or bothersome tasks no one else wanted to do. I was willing to do almost anything, but I wanted to be asked the way I would ask anyone else to do something for me. When the request from McNally became a command: "Rookie, pick this up," or "get that," "do this" or "do that," I balked. All he had to say was, "Fred, would you please give us a hand and carry the projector." I would have been glad to help. An approach of *asking me* rather than *telling me* may have made a tremendous difference in my relationship with him over the next 25 years.

Get Me to the Church on Time

I worked hard and especially studied the mechanics of the game. I wanted to be perfect. My goal was to be a referee. I started as a line judge and I wanted to be the best line judge in the NFL. Things I did off the field created problems for me with the league. Art was a devout Roman Catholic. He and the entire officiating crew went to church every Sunday before a game as did a number of the other officiating crews. We always went to a Roman Catholic church because few protestant churches had an early service.

In the middle of my second season, Art asked me if I would be interested in becoming a Catholic. I thanked him and said: "No." I did tell him that I would like to take communion during the service. He told me that it was impossible for me to take communion in the Roman Catholic church because I was not a member. However, the next Sunday when we were in church together, I walked behind him to the altar to take communion and kneeled. When the priest offered me the wafer, I took it. Since I was baptized and had taken communion in other churches, I didn't see any problem. I knew Art would be mad, but I took communion anyway because I felt no one could tell me what I could or could not do. This really offended Art, but I knew God didn't mind. In 1998, President Clinton was criticized by several Cardinals in this country for taking communion at The Vatican from Pope John Paul II because he was not a Catholic.

Another Sunday that season we were at church and had given money at the regular offering. Later in the service, the ushers came by again asking for money for the church building fund. Again, we reached into our pocket. The third time the priest asked for an offering during the service, Fred Swearington, our field judge, said: "Grab your wallets, boys, they're going to frisk us!"

In 1968, Mark Duncan, the supervisor of officials and the person who interviewed me and hired me to work in the NFL, left to join the management of the Seattle Seahawks. McNally was named to replace him and became the overseer of all officials for the next 22 years.

My Move to Referee

In 1970, my fifth season, Art called me and asked if I wanted to be a referee. Of course I wanted to be a referee. I started officiating as a referee and had always been a referee until joining the NFL. Almost no one comes into the league as a referee. When Art asked me to think about my decision, I told him I didn't need to, I wanted the job. I knew I was being recognized and rewarded for doing an outstanding job as a line judge. He still thought I should think about the move and call him back the next day. I did, and accepted his offer. For the next 19 football seasons I was the referee on the field leading my crew.

> *Fred was an excellent official on the field but his drum had a different beat. I liked working with him but you never knew what to expect. In a regimented business he didn't help himself, but Fred was always Fred, a little*

unconventional. Too bad he wasn't appreciated.–Robert
Moore, NFL back judge for 13 years and now a judge.

Less than a week before Christmas that year, Art called me and said I had been assigned to be the line judge for a playoff game. This would have been my first post-season game in the NFL, and after only five seasons. Playoff and Super Bowl officials are chosen by position and not by teams. I had to be rated one of the top line judges in the league to be given this assignment.

Christmas is one of the most important holidays in the year for me and my family, especially since I had been out of town every weekend for the previous four months. We had plans. On top of it all, my wife, Dolores, was sick and my children Kim, 15, Freddie, 13 and Scott, 11 years old, were looking forward to me being home.

I did what many considered unthinkable. I told Art: "No." My contract with the league did not permit me to turn down an assignment. He could have fired me on the spot. There are nine million guys out there who would jump at the chance I was given–to officiate an NFL playoff game. Ask any official in the league and most would agree that being away from the family at Christmas is a sacrifice, but no sacrifice is too great to be part of an NFL playoff game. I look back and remember that Sandy Koufax would not pitch on high Jewish holidays, even when the Los Angeles Dodgers were in the World Series.

It is unusual for anyone to turn down a playoff assignment. It had no effect on Fred getting another assignment. If he turned a playoff game down a second time, it would not have been wise and a totally different situation.–Art McNally, 10 years an NFL official and supervisor of officials from 1968 until 1990.

My response to the league's supervisor of officials was equivalent to shooting myself in the head as far as my future NFL career was concerned. It would be 10 years before I was again assigned to a playoff game when I would be in my 15th season.

You can't control circumstances, only how you react to circumstances.–Fred Wyant

A Contrast In Management Styles

I've always been self-reliant and independent. As a college quarterback I called all of the plays. Only twice in four years did my coach send a play in from the sideline. Our offense was the T-formation option. I was faced with several split-second decisions on every running play–whether to hand off to the fullback or a halfback; whether to pitch the ball out to a halfback going wide around end, or keep and run the ball myself. As the play unfolded, I had to decide what to do on every option. Our objective was to gain yardage, make first downs, score touchdowns and win the game. How we did that was my decision. Art McNally would say: "do 'a', do 'b', do 'c', do 'd' and you will get to 'e.'" I would get to "e" but I might skip "a," jump to "d," go back to "b" and skip "c." Add to this my management philosophy as an entrepreneur and self-employed principal with my own business. I was my own boss.

> *Fred was an official's official. He lived it. He was a fine referee.*
> *He was serious on the field. But he is going to do exactly*
> *what he wants to do. Nobody will intimidate him. He really,*
> *really, really enjoyed what he was doing.*–Jack Fette, NFL
> line judge 23 years, five Super Bowls, instant replay official

Contrast this with my new boss, Art McNally, who was a health and physical education teacher at Central High School in North Philadelphia, highly disciplined and in an environment where everything was done by a lesson plan and by the book. I never thought he was happy or a person who thoroughly enjoyed life. Getting me to conform to league policy was like trying to put a square peg in a round hole. I studied, mastered and always enforced the rules of the game. How I organized, motivated and worked with members of my officiating team I felt was my business.

I always enjoyed working with Fred. He is so easy to get along with and was always the life of the party.–Ralph Morcroft, NFL umpire for 20 years.

As a referee I had added responsibilities. The NFL referees were like Art's lieutenants and he was the colonel with Commissioner Rozelle being the general. Following weekend games, every Monday we called New York to report on what took place during the game–unusual plays, situations or problems. Later Art developed a form for us to complete to give the league the information they wanted. During the week we continued to study the rules and later the league would send us weekly quizzes.

Fred always kept us loose. We were relaxed and concentrated on the game.–Ed Marion, NFL headlinesman for 28 years and executive director and president of the officials association for 25 years.

I believe in participatory management. I want everybody around me to give me their ideas and let me know how they feel about my ideas. You can't control and hammer people all of the time and expect good productivity or creativity. Art was a control freak. He wanted the referee to be in complete control at all times. Our styles differed greatly. This is best illustrated by a Monday night television game when Cleveland played at Cincinnati early one September. On a passing play, the wide receiver came out and had some action with the defensive back. Jerry Bergman, my head linesman throws a flag. As he comes in to tell me why he called the penalty, Jerry says: "I've got an illegal cut." Then Donnie Orr, my field judge and a former quarterback at Vanderbilt, comes up and says he agrees with the call. But then Bill Carrollo, my side judge and in his rookie year, tells us he thought the wide receiver was his man to cover and that he didn't see any penalty.

I agreed with Bill, but I had two veteran officials telling me otherwise. Jerry is the greatest rules guy there is and had just officiated the Super Bowl in January. I ask myself, "Why am I arguing with him?" But

Donnie say, "Fred, Berggie is right." Now I have someone who has been with me 12 years and in the league for 19, telling me I'm wrong. But then Carrollo chimes in: "Fred, I think you're right and explains why." Bergman walks away, turns and yells back: "Fred, you're absolutely right." On television this must have seemed an hour for viewers, and like: "What in %^&$ are the officials doing?" The decision we made, as a team, was the right decision.

> *That was a major play in my career—national television, controversy and two senior officials who really knew the rules disagreed with me. I didn't feel I was in any position to question anybody, but I kept insisting, prolonged the discussion and couldn't understand why it was a foul. We picked up the flag. My call was correct. Sometimes if you're persistent and lucky you come up with the right decision. The next morning, McNally was on the phone to Fred.–*
> Bill Carrollo, side judge for eight years and now a referee.
>
> *We try to minimize conferences on the field. We have them because officials have different perspectives. If we have a discussion we can have a better look at it and be correct on the play.*–John Keck, NFL umpire for 25 years.

I took the full anger from McNally the next day. He thought I should have made an immediate decision, even if I was wrong, and to not delay the game by involving the other members of my team. He felt I made the league look bad on television. I told him: "Art, if you are in a management position are you going to dismiss the recommendations of two people with more than 40 years' experience?" I let him know that I wanted my guys to have a say in the final decision regardless how we looked. We had to be sure we were right.

> *Fred was the way he was. Good referees know they are in charge and you welcome contributions from everyone. More than any other referee, Fred welcomed contributions and discussions.*–Art McNally

Fred delegated different things to people, such as running our pre-game conference. The league frowned on this. To the NFL, the referee is the supreme being and supposed to walk on water. Fred didn't look at it that way. He wanted everyone involved. They didn't appreciate his management style.–Jerry Bergman, an NFL headlinesman for 30 years.

In addition to the Monday call, I had to call Art on Fridays between 9:00 and 11:00 in the morning to get game assignments for the following weekend. I also would be told of anything unusual to expect from the two teams whose game we would be officiating, including an interpretation of rules that needed review, a trick play to anticipate or other information that would be helpful. Art was so knowledgeable about the rules that he always had an answer for you. You were never not given an answer or left hanging.

Family First

Here is where I made another mistake. One Friday I decided to take off from work, be with my wife and look for a new family car. My son had a new motorcycle and Dolores and I had never ridden one. I completely forgot about my Friday morning call to the league office. It was a beautiful fall day, the West Virginia scenery was magnificent and Dolores and I had a great day. We got home at 6:30 that night. As soon as we walked in the front door, my son Scott said: "Mr. McNally asked you to call the minute you got home." Art was furious. He told me it was inexcusable to forget the call, that I was irresponsible and that I wasn't interested enough to be an NFL official. I admitted making a mistake by not making the call and said it still had nothing to do with my ability to do my job for the NFL and be a good referee on the field. The day I spent with my wife was far more important to me than making the call.

A happy person will not allow someone else to ruin his or her day.–Fred Wyant

Despite the way he operated, as a very loose individual, one thing I knew for sure about Fred, was that when the game started, he was in charge and was going to do a good job. He was all business.–Art McNally

During our annual pre-season clinic in my 10th year, those of us who had been in the league 10 years were to be given NFL rings commemorating our service. The meeting was in Pittsburgh at 8:00 in the morning. I had an important business meeting I couldn't change. It lasted until 2:30 in the morning. I was faced with two options: tired as I was, to drive to Pittsburgh and be there for the meeting, or go home and get several hours sleep and get up early. My alarm fails me–it doesn't go off. I wake up five minutes before eight. By the time I get to the meeting, Art and my colleagues are ready for a break. As I walk in, other officials, kidding, yell: "Hey, Art, Fred just got here!"

He was usually the last guy to arrive at our clinics, even when the city was closest to his home."–Ed Marion

During the break, I made a point of telling Art what happened, that my intentions were good and it was one of those things that happened. He was very angry. When I became a referee, he assigned Joe Connell, a very experience umpire, to my crew, to look after me. Joe and I got along great. First Art threatened to take Joe away from me to "penalize" me. Then he just handed me my 10-year ring, saying: "Here's your ring, Fred." All of the others who were being recognized were given their 10-year rings in front of everyone at the meeting.

I was boiling. This clinic had been scheduled for four months. It was extremely important and he knew it. I would put up with some things, especially those trivial, but nothing like this. He knew I was hot.–Art McNally

You have to love what you do. The day you stop love officiating, you have to get out. To love something, you have to have fun doing it.–Bama Glass, line judge for 16 years

People used to accuse me of doing things to deliberately antagonize McNally. He was the single individual who could decide the fate of my career as an NFL referee. I guess I couldn't help it because I was such a fun loving person. Any comedian would have loved to have Art McNally as a straight man. He was so uptight all of the time, he played the role perfectly.

> *Fred had a great flair for baiting Art. He would ask an irrelevant, off-the-wall question and pretend to be very serious. When Art got exasperated, then Fred knew he had him. He probably didn't do himself a lot of good with the league by doing those things, but it was a harmless side of his personality. He had an ability to keep you loose. At times that is very good.*–Gordon McCarter, official for 29 years, 21 as a referee.

During all the years I was in the league no official had any facial hair, except for a couple of African Americans who had moustaches. It was probably an "unwritten" policy from the league office. I started growing a beard in January. By the time of our annual pre-season clinic, it was full and completely covered my face. When I walked in the meeting room, everyone went berserk. Many, who were simply McNally clones, didn't know how to react. Later Art asked me if I was planning to wear it during the season. I told him I would shave it off before the first pre-season game.

> *I had another incident with a field judge from California who showed up at one of our clinics with a moustache and goatee. The night before the clinic we had a hospitality hour. I ran into him as we were going into the room and asked him how many pre-season games he had scheduled this year. In those days we had six. He said he had five. I*

told him fine, enjoy those five games. He got the message and was clean shaven the next morning.–Art McNally

The Class Clown

For our pre-season clinics, the meeting rooms generally were set up classroom style with desks. Most of the time I sat in the front row. At a meeting in Denver, my feet were killing me because of a rash or fungus. I took off my shoes and socks and put them on the desk. I knew the air also would help the healing process as long as it didn't bother my fellow officials. It didn't bother them, but it sure did bother Art. "Get your feet off the table," he yelled at me.

> *McNally just lost it. He chewed Fred out in front of everybody. But as soon as he did, it was over. That's the way he was. He never held a grudge.*–Red Cashion, 25 years as an NFL official, twice refereed the Super Bowl.
>
> *Fred was always joking. Art was a firm leader and has a pretty good sense of humor himself. This time Art hit the ceiling and was ready to chase him out of the meeting. But I believe Art got a kick out of it himself.*–Nick Skorich, a supervisor of officials for 22 years and now an evaluator.
>
> *He almost lost his shoes right there. I felt like going over and flipping his chair over as he was leaning back. My style was to deal with something when it happened and lay down the law. Once a person understands, it's history and gone. Forget about it and get back to business. Never berate someone about an incident again and again.*–Art McNally

During the break, almost everyone came up to me and said they felt Art's remarks were uncalled for. Later that day when we were getting our official league pictures taken, I probably exacerbated the situation because I came up behind Art, put my arm around him and told the photographer: "Art wants his picture taken with me." Of course that got a laugh from everyone but Art who jerked away from me.

Some people who have seen our interaction look at Art as the stern, strict and unforgiving teacher and me as the bratty student who gets the work done and gets high marks when the teacher wishes he would fail.

> *The very next day we took a side trip to the Bronco training camp in Greeley, Colorado. The day ran longer than we thought and a number of Catholics wanted to get to mass. We had two buses. One was going to our hotel and the other to church. Art wanted to fill both buses, but one was overloaded going directly to the hotel. Art asked if anyone else would like to go to church. Fred jumped up and said: Art, I'll go on one condition–if I can go to mass barefoot! That time McNally just laughed.*–Red Cashion

Art was running a meeting in St. Louis that he so dominated, no one else talked. Like other meetings, seldom would he call on an assistant or anyone else on his staff. He was being very repetitious and I saw no need to take notes. I'm glad I have great peripheral vision. All of a sudden I saw an eraser coming at me and ducked just in time. He had thrown the eraser at me in anger and then yelled: "Pick up the pencil and write." I looked at him and said: "When you have something important to say, I will write."

> *We used to bring in our rookies and put them with senior officials like Fred. Our veterans would work with the rookies giving them tips how to avoid troubles. I saw every one in the group taking notes but Fred, who was just sitting there. He was a free spirit and his attention might wander off. I had to bring him back to reality. I leaned over and said 'Do you want to stay in this league? Better get a piece of paper!' It was typical of him.*–Art McNally
>
> *Each issue was based on its own with Art. Nothing ever carried over. Once it was over, it was over.*–Jack Fette

I have been strong on the use of management and motivational tapes and have done extensive speaking on these subjects. I asked Art to consider using some of the management tapes for his staff in New York. I thought it might help give them a different insight into our jobs. He agreed to talk to others about it, but turned down the idea, even though others thought my suggestion was one he should pursue. I wanted him to be a better manager because it would make my life easier.

> *Don't ever have a great idea and take it to a negative person.–* Fred Wyant
>> *Much to my chagrin, Fred almost always sat in the front row. On the positive side, however, it was a place where I could keep my eye on him.–*Art McNally

This Is Haute Couture?

Another season the league changed the types of caps we wore from exact size, fitted caps, to the less expensive adjustable caps with a hole in the back. Most of us hated the new style caps. We felt we didn't look as professional with our hair sticking out the back. Before one game, I had long hair and put it in a pony tail and pulled it through the hole in the back. Art came into our dressing room, took one look at me and turned around and left. I think he got the message loud and clear.

> *Every year the officials would have discussions with the league office about money, expenses and uniforms. One year they asked the league to provide caps. Before this, the officials were responsible and bought their own caps. Commissioner Rozelle approved four for each of the officials. I didn't want to get sizes from more than 100 people, so I ordered 450 caps with adjustable sizes. It was a management decision for convenience, but it was a horrible mistake. We went to a very good company and bought quality caps. However, during clinics in Washington, D.C. and Denver, the officials said it was the greatest insult in the world to them because they didn't consider adjustable caps to be of*

the same quality. Fred, in his own inimitable way, let me know how much he disagreed with my command decision by sticking his pony tail through the hole.–Art McNally

After many complaints, Art rescinded the order. A week later we were in our dressing room at Veterans Stadium in Philadelphia and I put a sign on the wall, "McNally's Greatest Mistake Ever." Jerry Bergman was nailing one of the caps to the ceiling when Art walked in. I walked over to him, put my arm around him and said: "I thought selecting that adjustable cap was one of the best ideas you ever had. I loved that cap and would like to wear it today."

I refused to wear the adjustable cap. Fred didn't enforce the policy, even though as a referee he is responsible for inspecting us to make sure we are in proper uniform. On a televised game when I wore what I wasn't supposed to wear, Fred caught hell for it.–Jerry Bergman

The situation got so bad that when other members of our staff came back from games they would tell us how they got hammered by the officials over the caps. It finally got to the point where I agreed it was a bad mistake on my part and got all sizes from the officials and ordered new caps. Jerry Bergman's on the dressing room ceiling at Vets Stadium is a memento of the terrible cap that McNally had foisted on them."–Art McNally

Having fun in the dressing room before a game is important. To me, it helps us go on the field relaxed and be able to do our jobs better. Art and the league did not agree. I was assigned to referee the Pro-Bowl one year and was kidding with Tommy Hensley, the umpire on my team for many years. The alternate official in the room was complaining about not getting any playoff games. Again, my hair was long. I needed a haircut, so I took out a rubber band and pulled my hair into a pony tail. I had my front teeth knocked out in college in the days before protective face bars, so I took out my bridge. I flipped up the bill on my cap and started to make jokes, when Art walked in the room. I tried to grab the rubber band out of the pony tail and my fingers got stuck in the band. He just looked at me, turned around and walked out.

> *The league office was after him to get a haircut. He let it grow to the point where it was sticking out.*–Ed Marion
>
> *McNally and members of his staff would come into the dressing before a game and be as uptight as the head coaches. Fred would be doing his antics. No one took officiating more serious than Fred. He had an ability to come up with the right thing at the right moment to bring someone into focus and relieve tension. This kept his crew loose without stress and jitters.*–Gordon McCarter
>
> *I give the referees a lot of levity in dealing with their crews before a game. Most meetings are very well structured and a high percentage of business all the time. I knew that when he went on the field, Fred would be all business and he and his crew would do a good job. Under those circumstances, I was willing to go along with some of the things he did. If someone else did them they would be totally out of sphere. But this was Fred. He was unusual.*–Art McNally

Whether intentional or deliberate on my part, or just something that happened spontaneously, Art was fun to joke with. Jerry Bergman, our crew and I had been in Philadelphia for a game that ran late. Police acting as security for us knew we were going to have a problem getting to the airport in time to make our flights. They offered to help get us get there on time. We didn't ask for their help, but they volunteered to give us a police escort. Big problems arose when the Eagles' management heard about it and complained to the league office. I was criticized for accepting the help, even though we all would have missed our flights if the Philly police hadn't shown that "brotherly love."

> *This is very commonplace today. It is a sign of the times. To provide this kind of escort in those days was an absolute*

> *'no.' Today we help our officials get through difficult spaces and often with assistance out of the stadium and out of traffic.*–Art McNally

The following week we were in Cincinnati. In every city, someone always looks after us in our dressing room–helping with minor errands, interfacing with security and preparing food for us that can range from crab cakes in Baltimore to cheese steaks in Philadelphia. This day the attendant had prepared soup. Jerry and I knew Art would come in before the game to meet with us. We talked to the attendant and, unbeknown to him, involved him as part of a joke we wanted to pull. As Art went to get some soup, Jerry and I continued to get dressed, and the attendant said: "Mr. Mackuhnally, what time do you want your police escort?"

> *Fred's biggest downfall was his lack of seriousness before a game. He was a nonconformist. Absolutely. But once the ball was teed up for the kickoff, I don't think there was any better official in the league.*–Dale Hamer, NFL official since 1978.

Art exploded like an erupting volcano. No one in the room could contain their laughter. He came at Jerry and me, got in our faces and yelled: "What time do you get your game face on?" We smiled and calmly responded: "Five minutes before kickoff." This wasn't what he wanted to hear or see.

Praying for Help

Church again created a problem for Art and me. The officials' teams always meet the day before a game. Art said he wanted to join us at our Saturday meeting prior to a game in Atlanta. He wanted to go to church, which happened to be at the same time as I scheduled our meeting. He didn't like my saying: "Church should not take precedence over the meeting."

*I think John Madden liked to have as much fun as Fred.
Our crew was at church before a game and in the pew behind
us was Madden and several of his Raider assistant coaches.
I wasn't Catholic and was never sure when to kneel and
when not to kneel. All of a sudden I looked left and right
and I was the only person sitting. Madden was right behind
me and as Bob Frederic leaned forward, he picked up his
coat and motioned for me to go along with his gag. As we
were leaving, Madden had the coat behind his back and it
wasn't until we were at the door leaving the church that
Bob realized he didn't have his coat. Madden asked him if
he was missing his coat and then said, I'll give it back to you
if you give me a break today."*–Don Wedge, back judge with
Wyant for several years, a referee for three years, and side
judge in Super Bowl XXII.

The following week we're in Pittsburgh. Nick Skorich, who was a former NFL player and coach, had been on McNally's staff as assistant supervisor of officials since 1975. He did have a sense of humor. He stopped me outside of our dressing room at Three Rivers Stadium and told me how angry Art was from the previous week and the mixup in times. I told Nick that we were there but Art never showed up. "But you know how he feels about you and how he gets," Nick said.

At a mid-season meeting of the referees and umpires in St. Louis, I happened to be talking with some other officials in the lobby when Nick Skorich walked in wearing a very bright, checkered sports coat. Before our meeting started, I turned to Art and asked him to make a statement about Nick's wardrobe. I added: "Somewhere in the United States there is a cold !@$#%^ horse in the barn tonight. Skorich was quick to respond: "You'll think it is a cold day somewhere in the United States when you see the games you and your crew will be officiating the last four weeks of the season." It was one of the coldest winters in years and our assignments were New England, New York, Buffalo and Chicago. He could have easily assigned us Miami, Tampa, Orlando or

New Orleans. We were lucky. Each week, prior to the game, the cities had sub-zero temperatures, but by game time the temperature warmed up to the mid-30s. While it was funny, it wasn't always good to laugh at such situations. This was like my being asked to clean the blackboards or write, on the blackboard, some 100 or more times, "I will not make my teacher angry."

> *I did have a very loud sport coat that was black, red and white, but it also was very good looking. I told Fred that we'd have to see how his assignments go the rest of the season with cities like Green Bay, Buffalo, New England. We all had a lot of laughs over that one.–Nick Skorich*

After 15 Years–My First Playoff Game

In spite of my attitude off the field and my management style, I must have been doing a lot of things right on the field. In my 15th year in the NFL, and 10 years after I was first given and turned down a playoff assignment, I got my chance to referee a playoff game–the AFC championship game between San Diego at Miami on January 2, 1982. I could not make a mistake. I felt tremendous pressure to be perfect.

The night before the game, I had a wonderful experience. I took a walk around our hotel in the warm Miami air and looking up, could see the sky filled with bright stars and the moon. I am a very spiritual person but not a religious person. I believe in God, but not Heaven or Hell nor sin or guilt. I also believe we are all an extension of God and have the power to enter another person's subconscious mind. In the peace and quiet of the evening, I thought to myself, "Hey, any one who has ever been in a tough situation like this, that would like to officiate this game with me tomorrow night, come on down."

I knew if I screwed up this game it might not only be the last playoff game I ever worked, but probably my last NFL game ever. It was a warm, humid Miami night. The night before, Nebraska lost to Clemson in the Orange Bowl. The field was not in the best of shape but the grounds crew painted it green so it looked great on television and to the fans in the stands.

I really got into the game and was fortunate to have my regular umpire, Tommy Hensley, and another friend I really trusted, Vince Jacobs, my regular back judge, as part of my team. I had not worked with and really didn't know the other officials assigned to my crew. So before the game I went to Tommy and Vince, whom I trusted, and said: "Vince, you take care of everything down the field. Tommy, you take care of everything on your line of scrimmage. I'll take care of everything on my line of scrimmage and I don't give a #$%^ what the other guys do." This probably was not fair to the other officials or the way the league would have wanted me to run the game. But the three of us were the only ones who knew. Trust is one of the biggest attributes you can have from someone. I knew the three of us could make sure the game was good. It was probably the best game I ever officiated. Our crew didn't make any mistakes. This also was a tribute to the other four members of our team and how great they were even though I had not involved them in our "inner circle."

San Diego did everything right and jumped off to an early 24-0 lead. Little did any of us realize how long and hard we were going to have to work that night.

> *After we returned a punt for a touchdown, I came back to the bench where everyone was celebrating. Charley Joiner was sitting on the bench by himself. I went over and asked: "CJ, what's wrong?" He replied: "You don't come to Miami and do this to a Don Shula team. The game is not over. We're going to be here all day." He called it.*–Kellen Winslow, NFL Hall of Fame tight end for San Diego.

With four seconds left and the game tied 38-38, Kellen Winslow, who caught 13 passes that night, got his right hand up high enough to deflect the ball on an attempted field goal and send the game into overtime. The Chargers won the toss and drove from their 13 to the Miami 8 yard line. With 9:15 left, on second-and-goal, Rolf Benirschke missed a 27-yard field goal. The teams exchanged possessions. With 11:27 left, on the Chargers' 17-yard-line, on fourth-and-two, von Schaman's 34-yard field goal attempt was again blocked. Behind Dan Fouts' passing, including a 38-yard completion to Charley Joiner, the Chargers moved the ball to the Miami 10. On first down, Benirschke kicked a 29-yard field goal for a 41-38 San Diego win.

> *When Joiner caught that pass to set up the winning field goal, I was on the sidelines for medical reasons. I was the motion man and lost 12 pounds during the game. But when I saw the ball on the 10, I ran on to the field as part of the field goal unit and said I'm going to be on the field for this. I don't want to watch when we win."*–Kellen Winslow

A lot happened that night in Miami. Early in the second half, I noticed there was a string across the playing field from the upper deck on one side to the upper deck on the other side. In the heat of the action, I stopped the game. The ball on a rocket may not have hit the string. I doubt if any punter could kick the ball high enough to have the string interfere with the game. But I felt the string should not be there. This was my judgment call. Commissioner Pete Rozelle was at the game and I wondered if he was thinking, "What is that referee, who is only in his first playoff game, doing stopping this important game?"

We were told that year by the league office that the officials who had the best game in the playoffs would be selected for the Super Bowl. Back in our hotel room getting ready for bed, I handed Tommy Hensley a note that read: "We have the Super Bowl." Tommy says: "No way!" I told him: "But Tommy, they said they give it to the best officials and our game was officiated perfectly." I believed the league office. I wanted to believe in someone. And I would have liked to have seen anyone have a better game than we did that night.

Whether Art liked me personally or not, I must have been doing everything right. I got a playoff game the next year, and then for five more years. I'm telling myself, "Well, I never compromised once on happiness and now I'm getting the games I always wanted.

In 1987, I had one of my best years ever in the league. I had only one or two errors for the entire season. During the regular season and pre-season, teams ran more than 3,400 plays so my percentage of error was somewhere between 0.0002 and 0.0005. You really can't get much better than that! I was sure this was going to be *the* year I would be given a Super Bowl. I would have mortgaged my house and bet everything I had that this was *my* year. Then Tony Veteri, my head linesman for several years and now in the league office, called and said they wanted me to be the *alternate* for a playoff game. I couldn't believe what I heard. Alternate? No! I want to be the referee for the playoff game and then the Super Bowl referee? Being an alternate is like kissing your sister. I was so let down. To even be an alternate official for a playoff game, much less the Super Bowl you have to be doing many things right. Some people don't even get to be alternates. I refereed playoff games in 1982, 1983 and 1984, but no Super Bowls.

> *To get a Super Bowl is very tough. You're competing with 15 others and have to be #1 in your position. I know there were times when Fred was #2 or #3. Just one hesitation or one delay on a call could be the difference. Even if he had nothing to do with the call, it could cost him the game.*–Bill Carrollo

Career Changes

In 1990, Jerry Seeman took over from Art McNally as supervisor of officials. In his first year he forced out 10 senior, experienced officials and replaced them with inexperienced rookies. That should have sent a signal to me. In the next six years there would be an unbelievable turnover of some 45 percent of the most experienced, senior officials leaving and being replaced by rookies, who need five years of experience to become an NFL official.

Ben Dreith, an NFL referee for 31 years who called three Super Bowl games and officiated in playoff games for 28 straight years, was being pressured to quit or move to the line judge position. In his entire officiating career he had always been a referee. In 1990, he applied for McNally's job. Later he took the league to court over age discrimination. He also filed a complaint with the Equal Employment Opportunity Commission.

> *Then no one ever worked over the age of 60. Since my lawsuit, officials can work as long as they want to work. During my interview in New York for the job of supervisor of officials, when they asked me how old I would be on my next birthday, I got up and walked out. I told them it was against the law to ask. At the time I was 59. The NFL and their six attorneys from three laws firms settled with me 10 days before the trial was to begin. When my attorneys asked for the lists of officials and how they were ranked, they were not listed alphabetically, but by age with my name at the top.*–Ben Dreith, NFL referee for 31 years and three Super Bowls.

The last season I worked as a referee, before being reassigned to line judge, we had our summer meeting in Dallas. Art was explaining how the grading system worked. It always came up during any discussion because a number of outstanding officials were dissatisfied that they didn't get a playoff game. Art told us: "One thing that makes me so proud is having so many of you guys come up to me and tell me to throw out the grading system, that we don't need it, and I should just select the people I want to work the playoffs and Super Bowl. And you'll know I'm fair and will do a great job."

No official ever knows exactly where he ranks from the league's rating and grading system. We are told we rank in the upper one-third, middle-one third, or bottom-one third of those in our position. If you figure in a good year you may only have one or two bad calls a season, with some 155 plays a game, 16 games plus pre-season, the error of difference is fractional. You are judged on the calls made as well as the mechanics of the game, such as being in position to see the call. Movies were graded and critiqued and the league kept track of mistakes, telling you they agreed or did not agree with a call. You know if you're going to work a Super Bowl that you can't have any more than three errors in the year.

> *We were told officials ranked #1 at their positions would be given the Super Bowl. From legal discovery as a result of my lawsuit against the league I had a chance to see all of the rankings. The league information ranked me #1 three years in a row but I never got three Super Bowls in a row. People who were ranked #1 were not chosen and some who were not at the top of the list were given that assignment. The league office did whatever they wanted to do.*–Ben Dreith

At this meeting, I'm again in the front row, thinking and looking around. People are either smiling at him and agreeing, "It sure sounds good to me, Art," or else being silent with their heads down. I raise my hand and Art acknowledges me: "Yes, Fred." I say: "I've been in the league 24 years and I've never ever heard one official say that you should be the sole person making the selection for the Super Bowl. Not one." There was dead silence. As he tried to respond, I say: "Art, you have 10 percent of the decision at the end of the season anyway. I've had 36 hours of college math and if the ratings are as close as you say, then 10 percent could change someone from first to last in a position."

> *You never went into a football game uptight with Fred. His pre-game meetings and discussion were positive. If you made a mistake the week before he was not critical but constructive. He was always working to help you do a better job. My rookie year and second year in the league were with Wyant and were the two best years I had in the NFL.*–Gene Carrabine, NFL line judge for three years, now an observer for the NFL and Big 10.

During the break, half of the referees were in little groups and looking at me. The other half are more fun loving. When I walked toward them, they said: "Get the &*^% away from us. We don't want Art to think you're our friend." No one protested.

In the 27 years I worked with Art or reported to him, only four or five times did he ever call me before a clinic to tell me that he and the league were not happy the way I was doing this or that, or what changes he wanted me to make. At a meeting in Washington, D.C., he asked me to meet with his staff to review how I had been working that season. I told him if there is something he wanted me to do on the field, or something else he wanted done, I would do it. However, I made it clear that if he wanted me to change the way I act around people or life in general, I would not do that. He began to apologize. When our conversation ended, several people on his staff told me they admired the way I spoke up to Art and did not compromise my personal beliefs. While we had our differences, especially in styles and approach to management, we are friends and there is no animosity at all between us. Some people may find that hard to believe. However, I did have fun pushing his buttons!

The Move Back to Line Judge

At the end of the 1989 season, Art called me and asked me to switch back to line judge. He said that the NFL wanted to name several new referees. I told him I didn't want to be a line judge and wanted to go out as a referee. I then felt I was on my way out of the league and it wasn't my decision. Art gave me an edict: "You either be a line judge or I don't have a position for you." Did my always speaking up and saying what I believed have anything to do with it? I would think that it did. Very much.

> The competition among referees to get a playoff or Super Bowl is very intense. Sometimes a veteran official can move to another position and be in a better position to get a playoff game.–Art McNally

At our first clinic after my move back to line judge, a lot of the guys came up and wanted to know how I felt. They were trying to see how I felt mentally about the situation. A couple of them who were swing officials who had worked with our crew, told me that they would have loved to have been on my crew full time. My response to everyone was: "I told Art that I wanted him to be on my crew and if not, then he could switch me to line judge. And that's what he did." Of course everyone laughed and got a kick out of that.

This wasn't a pleasant time for me. I had an injured foot which made it a little tough for me to run. When I switched, Art assured me that I would have plenty of time in the area of four or five years to get acclimated to be a line judge if that was what I wanted to do. That all changed when Jerry Seeman came in with his own agenda.

Some people in the NFL obviously didn't agree with McNally moving me from referee to line judge. I was surprised one morning when I got a call at home from the legendary Paul Brown, then coach of the Cincinnati Bengals. In all of the games I officiated we had never said anything more than a "hello." He remembered me from college. He drafted my close friend and West Virginia teammate, halfback Bobby Moss as one of his top picks. He asked me: "Fred, why were you moved to line judge? Was it your choice." I told him: "Coach, I can't answer why, but I will tell you that it was not my choice." He then asked me: "You don't get along well with that *&@#$%^! McNally, do you?" Brown was really angry. He did not like McNally and whether he pursued it further, I don't know.

I guess I did what Art wanted that year. At the end of the season I was given a playoff game as a line judge. "You really did a good job this year," Art told me when he called. I said: "Art, I'm a professional. Why wouldn't I do a good job?" He agreed: "Yes, Fred, you are." I don't think that was the answer he expected from me. But that was my last playoff game.

I thought my wife was kidding me when she said Paul Brown is on the phone for you. I figured it had to be another Paul Brown until his secretary asked me to hold for him. I had only known him professionally and we had a coach-

official relationship. He was angry about what was happening and wanted to hear my side of the story.–Ben Dreith

I always liked Art as an individual, but I don't believe he ever thought that I liked him. I was like a "brat" in his classroom that he couldn't control. When Jerry Seeman succeeded him, first he stayed on with the league grading films. I believe it was a mistake for Art to continue working for the league because he was as much of an expert as Seeman. Both were very much alike. During my first year as a line judge as the pre-season meeting, Seeman asked Art to give a presentation. Almost everyone left the room as soon as the meeting was over. I was still sitting at my desk going through notes when he walked by. I looked up and said: "Art, that was an excellent presentation." He looked at me and said: "Did you really think so." I was serious and meant what I said. His skill level was tops. We disagreed on management style. A lot of people didn't think I would ever say anything nice about him or do anything for him. They were wrong.

In 1992, Seeman said: "Fred, if you don't get a playoff game this year, we're not going to renew your contract for the following season." This was a no win situation. The decision was his as to who got playoff games. He had total control. There was no appeal. Using the playoff game as a requirement for contract renewal was only a ruse. He would usually have someone in his office, like Jack Reader, tell you that you didn't get a playoff game and that you had the option of retiring because league was not going to renew your contract. That was my last year. Whether I would have stayed much longer, I don't know. As difficult as things were between Art and me, they were many times worse with Seeman. What was surprising, however, is that when Seeman was a referee and whenever we were in Minneapolis, he would always come over to visit with me and my crew. As serious as he was, I believe he enjoyed the kind of camaraderie and spirit our crew enjoyed. We always welcomed him at our meals.

This wasn't what I had been told. I knew things had changed drastically with Seeman in charge. I didn't ask Art to intercede on my behalf because it probably wouldn't have done any good. Although, I think he probably would have done so because of what he told me when he asked me to make the switch from referee to line judge.

In 1996, Art McNally came to Morgantown to see West Virginia play Purdue. He was observing officials for the Big 10 and asked if we could get together. I like Art, I believe he likes me and we consider each other friends, in spite of all that happened. When we had disagreements in the past, any anger was over at that time. I believe we both had an enjoyable time and I look forward to his scouting trips to WVU. I talked about instant replay which he liked and I didn't. I also tried to get him to be one of my sales executives for Melaleuca, another new business I have been developing. Regardless of our different approach to managing a situation, we both wanted the same result–a perfect game!

Should I regret never refereeing a Super Bowl. Probably. But would I compromise my happiness to make it happen? Or change my personality? Resist that one practical joke? Or change my management style? No! Would I do things any differently if I were given another chance? Absolutely not.

CHAPTER II

The Team

My job as a referee is to make sure all seven officials on the field function as a team. The referee is the team leader– the CEO, the field general, the one who has absolute final say. The league office wanted us to be dictators with absolute control. That was not my management style. I wanted every member of my team to feel they had equal say in whatever decision we made. The most important thing we had to do was make sure the call was correct.

To the fans in the stands and the viewers at home watching television, this may seem to be a simple job–to be out on the field watching the greatest athletes in the world compete in the greatest game in the world, NFL football. But if you're a serious student of the game, then you need to know how a call is made, why a call is made, and who is making the call. Knowing this will help you have a better understanding of the game and you can enjoy it even more.

All officials must masters the rules. We study them before the season, during the season, and after the season. We have pre-season clinics to discuss new rules and rules changes. We are given tests during the year. We must be as proficient in knowing our rules as judges in our courts know the law. In addition to the rules, we also must know the *keys* and *mechanics* of the game. Keys are individual position responsibilities on each play and vary according to the offensive team's formation. The mechanics include knowing the keys and being in position to make the right call. For each offensive formation there are different keys. On each formation, each official will have 10 or 12 different keys to remember. You have one set for the typical pro set offense, another set for goal line plays, others for kickoffs, and various passing offenses such as a flood, double tight end, double flanker motion, double wing, and even field goal attempts.

We have to know the game and anticipate what will happen so we are in position to make a call. After we have done our job on one play, we may have only 15-20 seconds to quickly review in our minds the keys for the next play. In a typical game, this could be mentally reviewing anywhere between 1,500 and 2,000 situations. Your mind has to work like a computer. To be the best in the league at your position, you could only have from one to three mistakes during a season. And you were at risk nearly 3,000 times when the center snapped the ball. After a game I would be more worn out mentally than physically.

If you had the opportunity to see an NFL officials' training camp guide or read the league's Officials' Manual, you would see how much an official must learn and know to be the best. We had different formations to recognize, know coverage responsibilities for each, the different situations for running and passing plays to kickoffs and field goals and everything in between. Officiating at any level is difficult but it is especially challenging in the NFL, considered it is the highest level to attain.

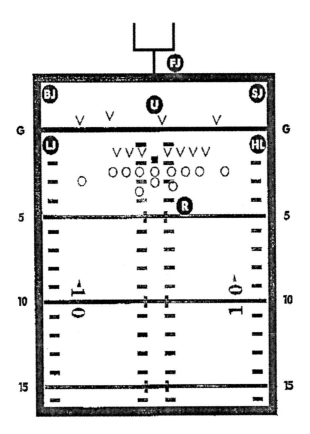

NFL Official's Manual, National Football League

This is the typical proset offense used by most teams in the NFL. The positions of the officials are indicated including the people they will be watching as the play starts.

There are also position responsibilities outlined by the league office. As a referee I had 27 during a game as well as others before and after the game. Some of mine included:

* The general oversight and control of the game and the final authority for the score and number of downs in case of a disagreement.

* The final decision on all matters not specifically placed under the jurisdiction of other officials.
* Prior to the kickoff to start each half and after every time out, I whistle for play to start. I didn't need to ask the team captains if they were ready and when I knew television had its allotted time, ready or not, I started the game.
* I needed to give the downfield men a chance to get back after an incomplete pass before I signaled the start of the 30-second count.
* I must personally notify the head coach and field captain when his team has used its three charged time outs. I also must personally inform the coach, in a positive way, of any disqualified player. I could not delegate this to any other official.

During the season, as a referee I had additional duties during the week that included the Monday and Friday calls to the supervisor of officials. The league outlined how the game day pre-game conference was to be handled, all of our pre-game duties and even had observers from McNally's office there to evaluate and critique us.

Once the pre-season started, I had to give up at least 20 straight weekends to the NFL. I would leave home to fly out Saturday morning to the site of the game for a pre-game meeting and, if lucky, would make flight connections to be home Sunday night with my family. It was a sacrifice. I did it for the love of the game and because I had fun and was with people I wanted to be with.

> *Successful people find few distinctions between work and play.*–Fred Wyant

Our crew started working together as a team during pre-season and then throughout the entire fall. Only when the most important games began–the playoffs leading to the Super Bowl–is the team split up. Then individuals considered the best at their positions are assigned to these games. Most have never worked together at all. When two teams are playing the most important game of the season, doesn't it make

sense to have the best *team* of officials on the field to control the game?
I would think so.

We were probably the only seven people in the stadium on a Sunday
afternoon who didn't care who won. We had no agenda. We had a job
to do and did it. It was lonesome being out there on the field in front of
so many people and knowing that someone was going to disagree with
everything you did.

If your team had a super season, chances were that the league
would split it up and send people strongest at their positions to weaker
officiating crews to make them stronger. This was wrong. The league
should leave its best teams in tact and work to strengthen the weaker
teams, but not at the expense of the best crews.

> *He taught me leadership and organizational skills. You have
> to understand him. You have to adjust, compromise and
> go with the personality of the crew. He was outgoing and
> relaxed, but when it came time for the kickoff, he was all
> business on the field. He didn't want anybody to blow a call
> by being uptight and nervous. That's something that can't
> be taught in a clinic or camp.*–Bill Carrollo

The first football officials didn't wear any kind of identification. Then
numbers were added to the uniform. Now you can tell officials by their
positions. This happened in the early 1980s because the coaches wanted
to identify which officials made which calls, especially if they disagreed
with a call and wanted to make a complaint.

Now the league has each wearing not only numbers, like the players,
but letters for their positions–R-referee, U-umpire, HL-head linesman,
LJ-line judge, BJ-back judge, SD-side judge and FJ-field judge. The
NLF's competition committee meets each year to discuss rules. These
meetings also can run as long as 12 or more days. The priority discussion
is to improve the game. And there is always talk about the officiating.

> *When a coach has a question about pass interference or
> another call, he wanted to know which official made the*

call. The line judge? Or the back judge? Or someone else on the crew? It was easiest to identify them by position. It also made it easier for the fans as well."–Art McNally

The referee wears a white cap and the other six officials wear white caps with black piping. This used to be just the reverse when the referee wore the black cap. When I first became an NFL official, I didn't wear number 11, my number as a quarterback at West Virginia University. I did get to wear number 11 later.

> *At one time all of the officials wore white hats. Larry McPhail, head of sports for CBS, used to always ask Mark Duncan, my predecessor as supervisor of officials, to put the referee in a different cap so the camera crews could search him out and be ready for his signal. It wasn't until later that we singled out the referee with a different type of hat.*–Art McNally

Until 1947, there were only four officials in the league. The back judge was added that year. In 1958 he was designated the official timer of the game. The line judge was added in 1965 and became the sixth official. He then took over the timing duties. That same year all of the officials' flags became bright gold. In 1978 the crew was expanded to seven with the addition of the side judge.

> *In the early 1980s, I recommended to the competition committee that the NFL referee use the same signals for the same penalties as are given in high school and college games. I felt it was confusing for the fans to see one signal on a Friday night or Saturday and then a different one on Sunday. Jerry Seeman changed the position designation of the field judge and back judge to coincide with the colleges. We always called our deep back the field judge and the back judge was on the side. Now it is just reversed.*–Art McNally

What most people don't know is the diversity of occupations represented on the field. NFL officials come from all walks of life. When I officiated, my colleagues included an oil company president, the chairman of an insurance company, president of a dairy processor, gas company district manager, bank president, stockbroker, financial consultant, mortgage company vice president, longshoreman, pharmacist, mayor, judge, attorneys, and many involved in all areas of education from teaching and coaching to being superintendents and principals.

We had a number of common disciplines and personality traits that included our dedication to our job, being able to make a decisive and quick decision, our professionalism, the ability to take charge and control difficult situations, being able to diffuse a crisis, and our innate sense of anticipation.

The Referee

My most important job was to protect the quarterback from injury. I decided when the quarterback was in the grasp of a defender. I enforced and controlled any roughness against him. The quarterback is the money player for his franchise. I think that being a former NFL quarterback gave me that gut instinct, which other league referees did not have, to actually know when the quarterback was in the grasp and to call the play dead.

> It was good to have a former NFL quarterback behind you. He understood what we were going through. Knowing him and knowing he played in this league, you know he is looking out for you. That makes a difference. Fred always did a very competent job."–Sonny Jurgensen, NFL Hall of Fame quarterback for the Washington Redskins.

I made a mistake in a game at Buffalo when I went too far with the team concept of helping out another official. As was my job, I was watching Denver quarterback Craig Morton. On one play, when no one was around him, I drifted off and watched as the play moved toward my line judge, Wilson Gosier. All of a sudden I heard a loud crash, turned around and Morton was on the ground, his helmet knocked off, and no one in sight. Morton slowly got up and said to me: "Where were you? Did you see that? I thought you were supposed to watch me!" I told him "Yes, I was." I never ever did that again. I always looked after my own territory first and foremost. The moment I took my eyes off of Morton, someone could have run a bulldozer over him.

My second most important duty was to keep television happy and work with the producer's assistant on the sidelines for commercial time outs. Television is money to the owners and the league. The way things are with the new owners today, I wouldn't be surprised if that is the number one priority. If a referee ran a game by-the-book as I did and didn't give concession after concession to the television network when the producer wasn't ready after a commercial break, and if the network complained, he might be in real trouble.

> *Fred was terrific on the field. He had an understanding and feel for the game and was one of the few that had many years of playing experience–not just in college, but professionally. My first year in the league, I was all ears, all eyes and wide open watching what he did. He gave me the motivation to hang in there and to be good enough someday to be a referee.*–Bill Carrollo

I positioned myself approximately 13-15 yards deep and directly behind the offensive tackle on the side of the quarterback's throwing arm. The NFL's guidelines said to be closer, only 8-10 yards deep. Being an engineering student for four years, I felt I had wider vision by being deeper and I could see more of what was happening on the field. When you see a referee get trapped in the game action or knocked down it is because he is too close to the action.

> *Fred Wyant could officiate a game better than anyone I ever worked with. He was the finest referee on the field–none better.*–Jerry Bergman

On every play, I watched the center, the quarterback's hands, the halfbacks, and the blocking. On a passing play, I dropped back with the quarterback, watched the linemen and when the quarterback's throwing arm is moving, I watched the direction the ball was moving to determine whether or not there was forward motion in the event he was hit. I was responsible to rule on possible roughing of the passer and if the ball became loose, to decide whether it was a fumble or a dead ball because of an incomplete pass.

On a running play, I watched the quarterback during and after the handoff and remained with him until action has cleared away and then move downfield with the ball carrier checking on him and the contact behind him. When the runner was downed, I determined forward progress from the nearest official on the sideline. I also watched the defensive line to make sure they were not illegally holding or pulling offensive linemen. I also determined when a first down measurement was necessary.

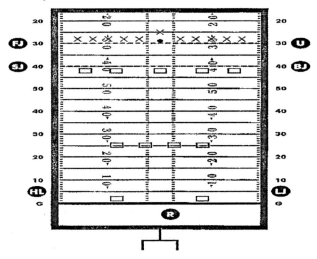

NFL Official's Manual, National Football League
Note the position of the seven officials on the kickoff.

On a punting play I needed to anticipate whether it was a clean snap. Did the ball come straight back to the punter without hitting the ground? I had to check to see if the defender ran into the kicker, or worse, roughed the kicker. Was the defender blocked into the kicker? Once the ball was punted, I followed the play down the field to watch for low blocks or clipping on the return. It was my responsibility to rule on running into the kicker or piling on the holder of a place-kicker.

You always had to watch what was going on with players away from the ball. You continue to officiate even though the ball is dead.

Umpire

The umpire is in the most dangerous position on the field. He is five yards behind the defensive guard and center on the side opposite the tight end. The defensive backs are behind him. League instructions tell umpires to not interfere with the vision of the defensive backs or their movements. All of the game action is coming right at the umpire in both directions. On a punting situation he drops back to about eight yards behind the center of the formation. If an official gets injured during a game, most often it is the umpire. This is one position I refused to officiate.

During the days of the first instant replay, the umpire was wired to communicate with the instant replay official in the press box.

The umpire watches the offensive line to make sure there is no movement before the ball is snapped, there is no illegal blocking or holding and whether an illegal lineman crossed the line of scrimmage prior to a pass. On a passing play he moves forward to the line of scrimmage as the play develops to be sure that interior linemen do not move illegally downfield. He also is responsible for checking the equipment of the players, must wipe down a wet ball and replace a muddy ball between downs, and helps keep players other than the captain away from the referee when he is explaining an option. On a field goal he becomes a double umpire with the side judge. On punt plays he moves to the offensive backfield approximately opposite the referee and observes the two guards, center and opposite upback.

Headlinesman

The headlinesman straddles the line of scrimmage on the sidelines or sometimes just outside the sidelines. He is in charge of the chain crew and gives them instructions 30 minutes prior to the game. In 1975 the league decided to have the chain crews uniformly attired, the ball boys clearly identified and required all clubs to use standard sideline markers.

He is primarily responsible for calling offsides, encroachment, any action pertaining to the scrimmage line prior to or at the snap of the ball, and any action involving a wide receiver's movement off the line of scrimmage. He uses his foot to mark the forward progress of the ball. When the ball is in his range, he marks out of bounds. The linesman also makes sure there are seven offensive linemen on the line of scrimmage and no more than 11 on the field when the ball is centered. He has to be aware of the eligible pass receivers on his side of the field and also any hooking and holding by the defense against pass receivers.

If the game action is coming at him, the headlinesman will not watch the ball carrier, but will focus on the blocking and the action in front of the ball carrier. If the ball goes out of bounds, he will mark the ball if it is in front of him and look out toward the crowd, in case someone is hit out of bounds. Every official has to be alert and aware of any infractions when the ball is dead.

The headlinesman assists in determining the forward progress by a runner on plays directed at the middle of the line or into his side zone and signals the referee or the umpire the forward point of the ball. He also checks with the referee regarding the down ready to start and, when asked, keeps the public address team member on the sidelines fully informed regarding any foul or incidents.

The NFL Official's Manual advises: "Do not be influenced by shouted comments from players or coaches on the side lines and do not allow them to perturb you." The most abuse I ever had was when I was a line judge because you are on the sidelines so close to a team bench. During my 27 years I was called every profane name you could imagine and some I never knew even existed.

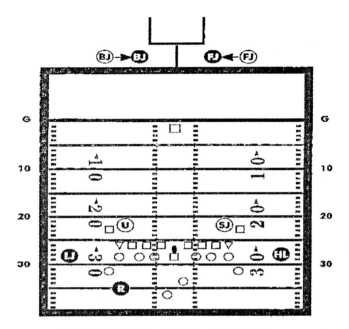

NFL Official's Manual, National Football League

On a field goal attempt the field judge and back judge move back to the goal posts to be able to see if the ball is within the uprights and over the goal.

Line Judge

The line judge was the first position I had in the league. It also was my last. I was a line judge for eight of my 27 years in the NFL. I consider this position the most difficult and most challenging because it has the most responsibilities. This is not the position you want to give a rookie. But the league did that more often than not.

The line judge straddles the line of scrimmage on the opposite side of the field from the head linesman. Except for the chain crew, he has virtually all of the other responsibilities regarding violations. He also rules the spot of a forward pass and whether it is legal or illegal as well and whether or not a lateral or backward pass behind the line of scrimmage is legal or illegal. He also protects the man in motion and watches to see whether he is legally or illegally in motion.

At one time, the line judge had the added responsibility of being the game's official time keeper. Today, the stadium game clock is official. However, in case it stops working or the scoreboard is not operating correctly, the line judge has to take over the official timing responsibility. He uses a football stop watch given him by the league. He must test the watch for accuracy before each game and keep a close check on the clock operator to make sure the scoreboard clock is operating properly.

Wilson Gosier, a former official in the World Football League and National Basketball Association and an outstanding college official, was in his rookie year and assigned to my crew. His college experience was as a side judge and back judge and he was one of the best in the business. To this day I cannot understand why the league did not build on his strength and bring him in as one of the back judges, rather than make him a line judge. And if stress isn't enough for a rookie, in his very first game in 1980, a pre-season game at Miami, the scoreboard clock went out and Wilson became the official timer.

> *During the second half I was on the sideline of the Miami bench. After every play Don Shula would ask me: "How much time do we have?"*–Wilson Gosier, former NFL, NBA, World Football League and major college official and a line judge for Wyant for four years.

The line judge also times each period and the intermission between halves. He signals the referee when two minutes are left in a half. He signals the referee and lets everyone know that time has expired at the end of a period by firing his pistol. It is his responsibility to notify the home team coach at least five minutes before the start of the second half.

What Would the NRA Say?

I worked a pre-season game with Frank Glover during his rookie year as a line judge. Before the end of the second quarter, he mistakenly fired the gun at the two-minute warning. I went over to remind him of the rules and said at the two-minute mark, you only blow your whistle. You wait until time has expired before firing the gun. As the clock was approaching two minutes in the fourth quarter. I again reminded Frank, "Now at two minutes, blow your whistle. Don't fire the gun. Wait until the game is over." I saw the clock go from 2:04, 2:03, 2:02, 2:01 and then heard the gun fire! I looked at Frank and he was terribly embarrassed.

We really kidded him unmercifully about that. Then when he was getting ready before a game, he accidentally fired the gun in the locker room. Talk about getting everybody jumpy and uptight before we went out to start the game.

Compare This to Any Other Line of Work

Here is how Art Holst, a line judge for 15 years with four championship games and two Super Bowls, describes what he has to look for in just a matter of seconds: "Before the ball is snapped, as the teams line up, do they have seven men on the line? Are all within one foot of the ball and not in the neutral zone, except for the center? Are all of the offensive players, including the backfield, set, with no movement, one second before the play starts? If a back is in motion, were all of the players set for one second before he goes in motion? Does anyone else move while the player is in motion? If so, all 11 must come to a stop again or there is an illegal shift. Does the center hitch the ball rather than making a complete swipe of the ball when he centers it? Does any lineman move his hand or have any kind of movement before the ball is snapped?

"You also are expected to keep time and does time run out before the ball is snapped? This is especially critical at the end of a half or the end of the game. When the ball is snapped and the quarterback throws a backward pass to a receiver, did he have possession, muff it or fumble it? What if the receiver picks up the ball and starts to run with it and then throws a pass beyond the line of scrimmage? Was the first pass a backwards pass and legal? Who now are the eligible receivers? Was anybody illegal before the pass was thrown? Then if another receiver catches the ball, is juggling it, but gets one foot on the ground, is the second foot in or out of bounds? As the receiver's feet touch the sideline, I blow a whistle and the receiver is then hit by a defensive man. Is it a late hit?"

These are typical of just a few of the mental decisions every official on the field has to make on every play.

Back Judge

This member of the team is behind the defensive backs and at the opposite end of the field from me. He is 25 yards from the line of scrimmage, deeper than any other officials on that side of the line of scrimmage, and positioned on the same side of the field as the line judge. He usually keys on the tight end and concentrates on his path to observe the legality of his potential blocks and actions the defense takes against him. He watches illegal use of the hands near the line of scrimmage and subsequent action downfield, pass interference and whether a pass is legally caught. The league told us to always rule a pass incomplete if there ever is a question.

The back judge has to be alert for substitutes entering the game before the center snaps the ball and watch for any players who take illegal positions without reporting. He is the "clean up" man on running plays which develop away from him. He has to watch for clipping, piling on and personal fouls before and after the ball becomes dead.

On fourth down punting situations, the back judge takes a deep position opposite the head linesman and behind and near the deepest receiver. If the line of scrimmage is inside the opponent's 50-yard-line, his side line position must be in the end zone in back of the pylon. He is responsible to watch for blocks in the vicinity where the catch is to be made. He also watches for clipping.

With two minutes left, he gives the two-minute warning to the head coach located on his side line. He asks the coach who will be the team captains for the remainder of the half.

On attempted field goals, the back judge should be on the end line 5-7 yards away from the closest goal post upright. When he determines the play is definitely going to be a field goal, he moves in close to the goal post to cover one of the uprights. If a punt develops, he immediately moves back to the side line away from the side judge and takes a position in back of the pylon. If the field goal is attempted, he and the field judge are responsible for letting the referee know if the kick is good.

In 1975 the league raised the goal post uprights to 30 feet above the crossbar and the following year attached a two-inch thick ribbon and 36 inches long to the top of each goal post to assist in determining wind direction. In 1978 this ribbon was increased to four inches wide and 42 inches long.

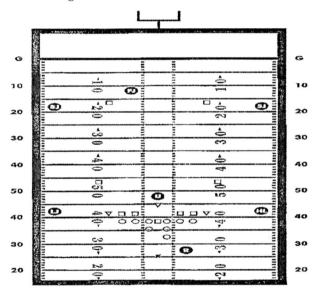

NFL Official's Manual, National Football League
Shown are the positions the officials take during a punting situation.

Side Judge

The side judge is on the opposite side of the field from the back judge, 20 yards from the line of scrimmage, and on the same side line as the head linesman. He is responsible for the widest receiver on his side of the field. He has many of the same assignments as the field judge, including watching for holding, pass interference, illegal substitutions and giving the coach on his side of the field the two-minute warning.

His primary responsibility is to decide on plays involving the sideline on his side of the field, such as a pass receiver or runner being in or out of bounds. He also assists in covering actions of the runner, including blocks by teammates and those of defenders, and rules on blocking during punt returns.

On field goals and point-after-kicks, he becomes a double umpire.

Field Judge

The field judge is on the same side of the field as the line judge and 20 yards from the line of scrimmage, deeper than any other officials on that side of the line of scrimmage. If he gets closer to the line of scrimmage he could be in the way of forward pass patterns. He is responsible for covering punts, forward passes crossing the defensive goal line and all loose balls out of the range of the other members of the crew.

Like the line judge, he also has a watch given him by the league office. Together with the clock operator, he times the 30 seconds a team is given to put the ball in play. He lets the visiting team coach know the time at least five minutes before the start of the second half.

He observes all player action downfield between the umpire and himself and assists me in any decision involving catching, recovery, out of bounds spot or illegal touching of a loose ball. He has absolute responsibility regarding the height of the tee used for kickoffs and instructs the kicker that the kickoff must be made by a placekick or drop kick.

On attempted field goals, the field judge is in the end zone a step or two beyond the goal line, with the back judge, watching for either a missed field goal or a fake field goal which results in the ball going out of bounds on his side of the field. With the back judge, he rules whether or not field goal and point-after-touchdown kick attempts are successful.

On punts he is behind and to the side of the receiver. He tells the punt receivers to be certain to get their hands up early and high for a fair catch. On attempted field goals he is behind the goal post with the back judge and covers one of the uprights to determine whether or not the kick is good. He also checks to see that there are not more than 11 defensive men on the field when the ball is snapped. He has to be especially alert to the television man on the side of the field to be sure I see his signals.

Teamwork

Teamwork is critical for us to do an outstanding job as a crew. The side judge, back judge and field judge have difficult jobs. There are a number of questions they have to ask themselves and be ready for quick, decisive answers. On a punt, did the receiver give a fair catch signal? Was it clear? Did the ball touch the defender and bounce off? Was someone blocked into the receiver?

On the pro set formation, when the offensive team gets set, each official has specific individuals he watches if there is a passing play. The assignments change if the offense has a double wing with halfbacks behind each tackle. Now the line judge watches the halfback on his side and the head linesman the halfback closest to him. However, if the offensive back closest to the line judge all of a sudden goes in motion in the direction of the head linesman, the two must instantly know they switch men. This must be done mentally, not like two defensive men who can call out to one another in basketball. Now the line judge has the man farthest from him. If this sounds confusing, how do you think it is to be an official on the field when the pro offenses are designed to be moving, changing all of the time prior to the team being set and the ball snapped. It is very difficult for the officials on the field to sometimes follow their men on a pass play.

Now take the pro set double wing. The side judge takes the wide receiver on his side of the field, the field judge watches the tight end and the back judge watches the wide receiver on his side. If one receiver on the line of scrimmage goes in motion, the decision as to who takes what man can't be determined until the ball is centered. The linesmen and the three back judges can't communicate verbally when they need to call for a switch. That is why I stressed basic fundamentals. It has to be automatic.

I believe it is important to work with the same officials every week. You grow together over the season. You need to constantly talk about mechanics. My goal was to bring the people on my team together so they were coordinated regardless of what developed on the field. As a team, we became effective in functioning and moving as an entire, single unit and not as seven individuals. We were ready regardless what the offensive team did. This was not an easy procedure, but we were either good as a team or bad as a team. If I had a great game and we didn't function as a team, then it wasn't a good game. I can't recall ever thinking that as a team we ever had a bad game. This, to me, is a tribute to the officiating prowess of an NFL official.

> *When you don't have a good shot at a call, scan the other six members of the team for their reaction. This is the team concept.*–Bama Glass

At every pre-game meeting I went over mechanics of what we did on every play. These were our fundamentals. I believe in the success of coaches who stressed fundamentals–Vince Lombardi, George Halas and Tom Landry. Lombardi would practice running the sweep over and over and over again. I stressed fundamentals for every member of my team so they would become automatic to them on the field.

> *You never went into a game uptight with Fred. He had a positive approach to his pre-game meetings. If we reviewed mistakes, his criticism was always constructive. He always worked to help you. The best two years I had in the league were on his crew.*–Gene Carrabine, former NFL line judge.
>
> *I was a swing man on his crew for several years and was not with him every week. There was no need for me to review the tape of the game from the week before because I wasn't involved. One Saturday we were in Pittsburgh and as Fred was going over the tape with other members of the*

crew, I took a nap on the bed. When I was sound asleep,
Fred took all of the other officials out of the room. The
phone rang, I woke up, answered it and found I was alone.
Fred, as the caller, disguised his voice and said it was very
important to speak to Fred Wyant at that moment. I re-
plied that he was in the bathroom and couldn't be dis-
turbed. A few minutes later they all showed up back in the
room. The joke was on me.–Don Wedge

The league gave us written instructions and let us know verbally what they believed to be the main objectives of the pre-game conference–to review the basic principles of officiating as they could apply to the game we would be working that day. We were to go over situations that might create problems on the field. McNally singled me out in a summer pre-season clinic and asked me to tell everyone how I handled a pre-game meeting. I said that I started by going position-by-position asking each individual to tell our crew what they did in their position. "We don't want that," Art snapped at me. I replied, "Art, I've been in the league 15 years. What do you want?" Several colleagues told me they felt I was being insubordinate. I probably was.

Fred was always very laid back and kept everyone else the
same way. The other crews were totally different and
probably overly structured.–Ben Tompkins, NFL back judge
for 20 years, worked with Wyant one season.

Art's explanation of the way he wanted the pre-game conference to be run was for me to carry on the entire discussion, tell each official what they needed to do and be in complete control. There was no room for participation by anyone else until he decided that he wanted one official to discuss a certain rule. During the week, we had to write on a card and send in a rule to be discussed. I felt this was a step away from basic fundamentals and basic mechanics.

He never believed in taking tests and never spent a lot of time off the field preparing. He always ran an exceptionally good game. He knew the rules on the field whether he acted like it off the field or not.–John Keck

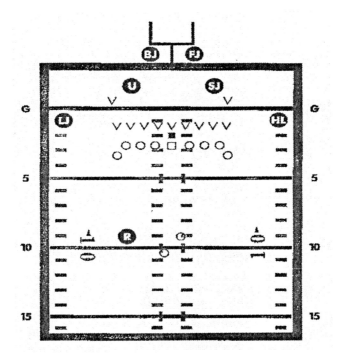

NFL Official's Manual, National Football League

Shown are the positions of the officials during a try by kick for a point after a touchdown.

When I worked with Fred and his crew one time in Pittsburgh, rather than meeting in a room, he told us to meet in the lobby at a specific time. We walked across the street to a park where Fred conducted the entire pre-game meeting as we leisurely strolled through the park. The next day we may have had the best game we ever had as a crew. Fred was something else!–Don Wedge

In the manual, the NFL at least gave me some latitude by writing: "Referees will undoubtedly vary in their approach to the pre-game conference. ... Referees and their crew can stress certain items and views throughout the meeting." My approach to management was to delegate authority and responsibility and let my team learn and grow. Participation and involvement are part of team building.

> *Fred was an excellent field official. He never got upset or let little things bother him. He never let our team get caught up or involved in situations like other officials did. For on field performance, our crew had games shorter than the league average and for the most part always free of conflict."*–Joe Haynes, line judge for nine years, six with Wyant, and the first African American to be the referee a game in the NFL

I believe this approach works to reduce stress. There is enough stress in our daily lives. Being an official, even more is added before you step out on the field. I wanted my team to be relaxed and have nothing interfere with their complete concentration on the game once it started.

> *When Fred was on my crew as line judge he always did things his way, but not the way the league wanted them done. However, he always got the job done. During one pre-game conference I asked Fred to go over the timing rules. His response was: 'each team gets three timeouts each half and you give each coach the two-minute warning. That's it.' With that, Stan Javie threw the rules book at him from across the room and yelled: 'Here ... read the *&*%$# book!' Fred was always so casual and laid back."*–Ben Dreith
>
> *Fred knew the basic rules on timeouts but there was so much more to know. He depended on his natural ability and the fact he had some terrific veterans on the team with him. I was always on him about studying the rules. I would regularly ask him questions about something specific to timing. I would get upset with him if he didn't know the*

answer. I wanted him to know the rules.–Stan Javie, NFL
back judge for 30 years and four Super Bowls

I ran my meetings the way I ran my business. The basic fundamentals
of marketing and selling don't change. Wasn't this the way of the great
coaches?

> *Fred had a reputation among officials of being able to keep
> his cool in a big game, late season game, or division title.
> His manner could put things into perspective–the right
> wise crack or a few chosen words at a moment when
> someone was getting up tight and stressed out, uptight,
> tense and susceptible to making an error. His way with
> people was an excellent trait. Sometimes this was
> misconstrued by the league office.*–Gordon McCarter

I felt that Art always had a difficult time coming into our dressing room
after a game. He would never tell us we had a great game because he
wanted to see the film first. But as a referee I knew our crew had a
great game. He should have given more praise to his officials than he
did. Officials who retired from being active on the field, and who, like
Art, went to work in the office of the supervisor of officials stopped
behaving as they did when they were on the field working the game.
They became very critical.

> *He was always consistent. Not a phony. Seldom was he
> politically correct. Art was the boss. You have to obey the
> boss. Fred and Art clashed all the time.*–Bill Carrollo

One my fellow referees, Jerry Seeman, now the league's supervisor of
officials, was very concerned that someone might hear what was being
discussed in the official's dressing room following a game. I believe he
felt there was going to be someone listening at the door–a coach, player,
member of the press or a "spy." Simply locking the door wasn't good
enough for him. He went so far as to actually tape the door shut so not

even air could get in or out of the dressing room. I used to kid Leo
Miles, who had been my head linesman before moving to Jerry's crew,
that to tell Seeman I trained him for taping. What kind of pressure did
that put on his crew?

> *Nothing bothered Fred. If he was more rigid, more
> commanding and ran his meeting with more discipline, he
> would have had a Super Bowl."*–Tony Veteri, official for 23
> years and eight years in the NFL's supervisor of official's
> office.

I believed that my job was to make sure my crew was always mentally
ready every week. I never minded someone pointing out something to
me if I was wrong. I could work on it and correct it. I hated it when
someone came in and jumped on someone on my team at a time they
needed to be stroked or supported. I don't believe people today have
fun officiating in the NFL.

> *Whatever he said you could take to the bank. He was not a
> politician but all business on the field.*–Fred Heichmer, NFL
> field judge for six years.

The Weekly Routine

During the season I had little time to devote to my business. Being a
referee was very demanding. I had my Monday morning calls. Then I
would have a weekly test on rules to complete and have to discuss for
our team meeting before the game. Friday I had to call again for
assignments. Saturday it was off again to the next city, unless we had a
Monday night game on television.

We started the season in early March when we received a 300-
question open-book exam on rules. I was lucky to be close to Pittsburgh
and in an area where there a number of my colleagues lived. We would
get together to discuss new rules, rules changes and interpretations.
When we went to our pre-season clinics, we would discuss those

questions where there was a lot of disagreement. Some people didn't agree with the right answer. We would discuss mechanics.

During the off-season, the league sent us film and later video highlights of calls we had made with a critique sheet. I had to reply with my own self-appraisal. During the summer meeting we would break into smaller groups by positions with the referees going off for a session and the same with the umpires, linesmen and judges. We would discuss how the league critiqued us, our self-appraisals and review certain plays. After that we would go out on a practice field and run sprints, laps and do physical exercise and training. The league also brought in their security and narcotics people to talk to us. I was always careful who I talked with. The league also had a rule of not drinking once an official left home to go to the game site until he was on the plane on his way back home after the game. I never drank at all. There are so many opportunities for someone to misunderstand what is reality. In today's world, perception is everything.

In my later years, the league began giving annual eye examinations. The first year the examinations were given, McNally was standing by the ophthalmologist and I was first in line. I couldn't resist doing something funny. When the doctor motioned for me to come forward, I deliberately did a Mack Sennett pratfall and walked right into the door jamb. Of course it brought the house down and even the eye doctor was laughing. But Art didn't think it was funny at all.

A great deal changed when Jerry Seeman took over from McNally. Some likened his summer meetings to a marine boot camp. The workouts at the meetings were very stringent. Someone said he started this to weed out nonconformists like me.

> He's [Seeman] very, very structured. His clinics are regimented. There's no room for discussion. There's too much emphasis on standing straight and tall.–Don Wedge, side judge for 24 years

Seeman now has three written tests. In March, two 75-item rules exams are sent out followed by a 200-question exam in April. A supervised written test is given at the pre-season clinic. In April we also received the video tape of penalty calls made during the previous year with positive and negative critique. Special meetings are held three or four times during the season involving the referee or umpire from each crew.

Do all of the timed wind sprints, shuttle races and exams guarantee the official is going to be in the right place at the right time to make the right call? I don't think so.

Working With the Media

As a referee I also had additional meetings with the league's public relations and media relations staff to talk about responsibilities with television and the media. These also are spelled out for us in our manual with two basic rules we had to keep in mind at all times:

1. Be courteous.
2. Your job is officiating. You are not a spokesman for the National Football League or any of its teams.

We were also told that at any time, except in the emotion-charged atmosphere of a game or its immediate aftermath, to explain and discuss a rule. We could not discuss a particular play, ruling or interpretation with the media in general.

> *I believe Art (McNally) was always worried that our team, collectively was going to do something that would embarrass the league.*–Jack Steffen, back judge for 10 years, several with Wyant

We had a controversial call in Chicago one Sunday which ended up in my getting pressured from the media for an answer. The Bears had the ball on third down with 18 yards to go and a penalty was called against the defense. I walked off 15 yards, gave Chicago the ball and replayed third down. I thought it just required replaying the down. Dick Hantack, now one of the best referees in the NFL, was one of my deep back officials and he came in to talk with Jerry Bergman and me about the call. Dick said he thought it was a loss of down. There I was with two of my most knowledgeable, senior officials. Berggie and I allowed Dick to convince us we were wrong. As it turned out, he was wrong. All three of us got marked down by the league office for the error. The worst of it came after the game when the reporters wanted an explanation.

> *Several of us told Fred it should have been an automatic first down for the Bears, who ended up not making the first down.*–Chuck McCallum

It was bad enough to have reporters, who don't have a clue about the rules or any understanding of them, asking questions when they wouldn't know how to interpret the answers. George Rennix, a retired referee who had a radio program was in the room and he kept trying to interrupt me. He knew we made a mistake and the reporters were right in their assessment of the call. I finally had to ask George to please be quiet, to go over in a corner, I would take care of the reporters and would talk with him later.

As I started giving an explanation no one would understand, I don't think George thought it was funny. It was all Hantack and Bergman could do to keep a straight face. Finally, as I was convincing the reporters we were right, they had to go around a corner of the locker room.

> *Fred's explanation had the reporters so confused that I don't believe even he had an idea of what happened.*–Chuck McCallum
>
> *By the time he finished with his explanation, the reporters were totally confused. Jerry and I were laughing so hard we had to leave. When they left the dressing room, some may not have even known they were at a football game. We should have given the Bears an automatic first down instead of replaying the down.*–Dick Hantack, 21 years in the NFL, the last 13 as a referee, worked playoff

games for 20 years and two Super Bowls, one as a back
judge and one as a referee.

The reporters eventually left shaking their heads. That was what officiating
in a tough league was all about. What I did was not a cover up. In a
game I have to match myself against the players and coaches. In this
instance it was the reporters covering the game. Dick, Jerry and I already
knew when the league looked at the film that we would be marked
down for the mistake. What I did didn't cost anyone anything.

So What!

Chicago's great running back Walter Payton had a habit of sliding
the ball forward after he was down, always trying to get a few more
inches on every run. In a game the Bears had at Atlanta, a defensive
player picked up the ball after Payton slide it forward. Ed Marion, my
head linesman, ruled it a fumble. The Bears were already in their huddle
ready to run their next play when Payton realized what had been called.
He charged Marion disputing the call. In the excitement, Payton put his
hands on Ed. When he touched him, every official seeing what happened
threw their flags and Payton was ejected from the game. On Monday,
the league ruled our crew had made a mistake. A sportswriter from
The Chicago Tribune called Ed at his home, told him the league said he
had blown the call and asked him for an explanation. I loved his response:
"So what!" After that McNally put a gag order on us.

> We were the only officiating crew to ever throw Walter
> Payton out of a game. And we blew the call. But following
> Ed Marion's response, we used to say 'So what!' a lot of
> times in our dressing room.–Wilson Gosier.

The hierarchy on Park Avenue gets very upset when officials speak out
without their permission. Chad Brown, an African-American umpire
found out the hard way in 1999. He wrote a book, *Inside the Meat*

Grinder, about his experiences. He not only was told not to do any media promotions for his publisher, but was fined $3,500!

Other Game Day Activities

We had to arrive at the stadium precisely two hours and fifteen minute before game time. When we did, the line judge went to the television truck to get the exact time. At two hours before kickoff, I had an on field check of all electronic equipment with my umpire and the designated club game day coordinator. When we had instant replay, the instant replay official was with us. The count down went on with what we were to do before, during and even after the game. Every member of the crew had responsibilities and assignments.

The Necessary Accessories

There are so many necessary items an official has to have on him I finally got around to making up a checklist so I wouldn't forget what I needed, ranging from a coin to toss to a flag, bean bags, whistle and rubber bands. Once, I walked on the field and realized I had left my whistle in the dressing room.

The American public learned in December 1999 all about the weighted yellow flag which is thrown for any penalty. During a game between the Cleveland Browns and Jacksonville Jaguars, referee Jeff Triplette threw his flag and it accidentally hit Cleveland tackle Orlando Brown in the eye. Triplette immediately rushed to Brown and apologized as he pulled the flag from between the face mask and helmet. Brown, who is 6-foot 7 and 350 pounds, left the field but then stormed back on the field and shoved Triplette, 6-foot 5 and 203 pounds, to the ground.

The incident prompted the NFL to review how officials throw flags. I have never seen the flag hurt someone, but have had my penalty flag get caught in a player's face mask. The league suspended Brown indefinitely. However, when you know that his father had lost his eyesight six years previously and this accident could end his playing career, it does explain, but not excuse, his anger.

I usually kept my yellow flag in my back pocket. We also had weighted bean bags which are thrown for a change of possession, to mark the point of a fumble, an interception, or where the ball is caught on a kickoff or punt. It is small and weighted on both ends so it can easily be carried on the belt. Some officials carry two bean bags.

Rubber bands are a must and used by all officials to keep track of downs. Many of us used to make up our own for systems we had but now some are more sophisticated in design with an elastic wrist band and attached rubber bands that could be moved from one finger to another.

We all had cards and pencils to mark down all penalties. Before the league came up with weather-proof cards, we used to keep them in plastic bags to protect against rain and snow. I kept all of these in a plastic bag with my checkoff list

The line judge also must have a stop watch since he is the official timekeeper.

Oh, That Weather!

The mailman talks about delivering mail through rain, wind, sleet and hail. We had all of that and worse. I had pneumonia five times in seven years. Being a chain pipe smoker at the time didn't help. I quit after I was sick the fifth time.

College officials can wear clear plastic raincoats over our officials' uniforms. This was not allowed in the NFL. Later the league did develop water proof shirts. My health was important and I did whatever it took to stay dry. I was the only official in the league who wore high top shoes. I did so because they not gave my ankles more support but were more comfortable. I knew the league didn't like it, but they never told me to change.

> There's no doubt Fred was a rebel. We were in New England
> and it was pouring rain. He didn't have proper rain gear and
> at halftime came out with a plastic jacket with 1" black and
> white stripes and the rest of us had our shirts, with 2"

stripes, neatly tucked in. Three minutes into the third quarter the observer came down from the press box, stopped the game and made him change.–Wilson Gosier.

Cold, sub-zero weather was another thing. We put Vaseline on our face. I started with a light pair of socks, then would cover them with a plastic baggie before putting on my official NFL outer socks. I needed to keep my feet not only warm, but dry. I usually wore Jockey shorts and had insulated underwear that I would cut for shorts, and then put on a layer of long insulated underwear before putting on my pants. Underneath my shirt I had a T-shirt, plastic or nylon long sleeve shirt, an insulated turtle-neck, a sweater or sweatshirt and then the insulated long sleeve official NFL striped outer uniform shirt.

My hat had ear muffs and I also wore black and white ski gear around my ears. When we all walked on the field we looked like Pillsbury Doughboys, but none of us cared. We wore black or white gloves like baseball batting gloves. Many of us also had hand warmers inside our gloves and in our pockets.

There are only 13 minutes of action in a game. The average play is over in six seconds. You are out there for anywhere from three to three-and-a-quarter hours and longer. Longer if the game goes into overtime. And it was even longer when we had instant replay. I was lucky and never got frost bitten. Fred Silva wasn't as lucky. He worked a playoff game in Cincinnati and flew in from California without any protective outerwear. His ears and hands were frostbitten. After that, Fred has never been able to work a game in cold weather.

The league has come a long ways working to develop and make available protective uniforms and equipment for the officials. We are the ones who need it the most. Players go to the bench for protection. We are subject to the most exposure and need to be in the best of health to manage the game. Who knows, maybe someday there will even be protective padding for the umpire!

CHAPTER III

Mistakes Do Happen

What a perfect world it would be if no one ever made a mistake. Would we really want life to be that way? I don't think so.

As officials, when we put on those zebra-striped shirts and walked on the football field, we were expected to be perfect. There was no room for error. Mistakes were made. But they were very few and far between.

Just consider the odds and the pressure for only 13 minutes of action. In a three-hour football game, that's all the action there is. There are 155 plays a game, including tries for extra points and those where penalties were called. Each official has to think about 10 or 12 or more keys before each play begins. You have about 15 or 20 seconds to do that before six seconds of action. Your mind has to be like a computer thinking about 1,550 to 1,860 options every game. For all seven of us on the field, that adds up to between 10,850 and 13,020 possibilities! After a game I would be mentally exhausted.

A season with four pre-season and 16 regular season games means you are at risk 3,100 times. When the best only make one or two errors in a season, that's an average of 0.0003 to 0.0006. Now for team statistics, divide that number by seven. The error percentage is so small it is infinitesimal. That's how very good officials are in the NFL. It's better than ninety nine and ninety nine one hundred percent pure!

Yet we do have those days. Have I ever seen a good official have a bad day? I would say no. Have I ever seen a good official miss a call. Yes. Have I ever missed a call? Yes.

> *In football the people expect you to be perfect. No one decision is more important than another. An offsides penalty against a team for five yards in the first quarter may seem insignificant, but it could have led to a first down and a touchdown. There is no such thing as an insignificant call in football. All are important.*–Art Holst

When you reach certain levels of professionalism in life, such as being a writer, coach, physician, surgeon, lawyer or scientist, you seldom are going to have a totally bad day unless you are mentally out of whack. Mistakes can happen.

Who would have ever thought the NFL would have to apologize to the Pittsburgh Steelers when officials made mistakes in three different games during the 2000 season? All were made by different crews. The Steelers lost all of the games, two by only the margin of a field goal, and one in overtime. A correct call could have put the Steelers into the playoffs.

Would you expect to see mistakes in some of our most important publications? Take *The Wall Street Journal,* for example. It is one of the nation's most widely circulated and read newspapers. A survey by Professional Proofreading Services reported that the May 28, 1998 final edition had an average of 4.73 errors per full page. That's not 4.73 errors for the entire edition, but per page! And things are not getting better, but getting worse. This was an increase in errors of 38 percent over the previous survey done in July 1996. Does this mean we can't believe all we read? Or hear on the radio? Or see on television?

Some erroneous media reports are not just typos. There are factual errors in reporting. All one has to do is look at the way television reported on the Florida voting results in the 2000 Bush-Gore Presidential election.

> *Any official who tells you he didn't have a bad call is lying.*– Tony Veteri

Fans don't believe anyone should ever make a mistake. Yet they happen in a football game. Officials grade out almost perfect. What about players? An overthrown pass, a missed block, a dropped pass, a fumble, or a missed tackle? Few grade out 100 percent after a game. Even the coaches call the wrong plays or have a wrong defensive adjustment. Even the radio and television announcers make mistakes–a slurred word, mispronounced name, or making a wrong call. They certainly do not always know the rules.

> *Don't allow someone to lay guilt on you, not even your preacher.*–Fred Wyant

We do know that calls get missed. Even some that are very obvious. Books have even been written about mistakes officials have made. But few have been written about the mistakes players, coaches and members of the media have made. Here are my reasons why I believe a call can be missed:

1. The official is not in position to make the right call.

> *If you are the primary coverage official and for whatever reason, you are out of position, it is not acceptable. There are exceptions in most avocations and vocations, but in officiating that's no excuse.*–Chuck McCallum, field judge for four years in the league, all with Wyant.

2. The official is in position and is either screened off from the action or caught up in the play itself and does not see the entire play. Great officials don't make a call if they don't see the entire play, even if a foul does occur.

> *If you're 5'9" and weigh 175 pounds, it is easy to get blocked out of the play or screened in the end zone by someone 6'8" and 290. I look for feet first in the end zone and then the ball for a touchdown. You also can be so close to the play that*

you can't see it. That's why you have a crew conference because someone farther away may have seen it better.-Art Holst

Sometimes you might have a bad angle and see the play differently. I've called them when I've been knocked on my butt. A coach saw me get hit and knocked down and yet I called the play. He said "How can you call it on your backside? But you got it right!"-Mike Lisetski, 18 years as a field judge, 18 years in the league office, worked the first Super Bowl and two championship games.

3. Judgment was wrong when a split-second decision was needed.

Fred was a stickler for getting it right. His umpire, Tom Hensley, kept him out of so much trouble. If one didn't have the answer, the other one did. Both were excellent. No one on the crew ever questioned their judgment.-Gene Carrabine, line judge for two years with Wyant.

4. The play happened and you weren't mentally prepared for a particular foul that happened. You immediately do an instant replay in your brain, which you can't do, and it is too late. You missed the call even if you were looking directly at it.

In 18 years in the NFL I never played a perfect game. If I could play a perfect game, I would have expected the officials to be perfect. But the game is played by humans and officiated by humans. Mistakes will be made.-Sonny Jurgensen, NFL Hall of Fame quarterback.

I have always been a student of happiness. I understand what I have to do to mentally prepare myself to be happy under any circumstance. When I was on the field, I would never be affected by something happening outside of the game. I put myself through mental processes before, during and after the game. For my team, I stressed mechanics.

To make the right call you have to anticipate what is going to happen and be in a position to see the action. It is impossible for seven officials to watch what 22 men are doing at any given moment.

A call can get missed because of lack of concentration.–Jack Fette

You get mentally prepared for the next play when the team is in the huddle. You ask yourself: "What down is it? What is the yardage?" You plug that in to expect a certain situation. What do I look for? It may be an obvious pass, but the quarterback could call a draw. As the referee, I wanted to be sure I could see the ball being handed off in case there was a fumble and to be certain the blocking was legal.

I was Fred's line judge the first year he was a referee. We had the Steelers at Miami. Pittsburgh punted on fourth down and a Miami defensive end got through and was blocked into the punter. A TV timeout was called and Don Shula was behind me and yelled, 'Wasn't that roughing the kicker?' I told him "no" because his end was blocked into the punter. He then came back, "Who's that ref? Number 11? Is he a new one?" I told him "yes." He then asked me, "Does he have the balls to make that kind of call?" Shula wasn't complaining, but was trying to find out what he could about Fred.–Art Holst

The defensive team has help with a staff of defensive coordinators supported with computer programs and experience ready to stop the offensive team. The next time you're at a game, or watching one on television, consider what is going through the mind of any given official waiting for a play to begin. NFL teams have the most sophisticated offensive formations. They are skillful in disguising what they plan to do. When the offense breaks from the huddle and lines up, you have less than five seconds to recognize the formation and know the player you will be watching when the ball is centered. It gets worse if you are one of the back judges and the receivers cross in front of other people, so an official on the left sideline had the receiver move to the right sideline, or vice versa.

We can't have officials running across the field, like defensive backs, or even yelling out "switch" on the coverage. This is where teamwork and mechanics become so important. If you were unlucky and didn't cover everything you needed to in your mind before the ball was snapped, you could be so surprised that you were both physically and mentally out of position when the action happened, and the play was over too quickly for you to make a call.

If you're not in position, 90 percent of the time you'll make the wrong call. You need to be 99 percent correct and must be in the right position. You have to know the mechanics.– Bama Glass

Counting Downs and Players

One of the worst fears of any official is to miss a down and give the other team an extra play, or take one away from a team. One thing every member of my team constantly did was to put up fingers for every other official to see denoting the down–one, two, three or four. We each had our own way of keeping track. Some used rubber bands to various devices on fingers. If we ever were not in 100 percent agreement we would go upstairs to the play-by-play official for confirmation. This never happened in my 27 years of officiating but has happened in the league.

The headlinesman has primary responsibility for the box marking the downs. You would wonder with television, the scoreboard and officials how a down could be missed. Sometimes a penalty can create confusion on the field regarding a particular call and it does happen in a football game.

When certain calls are flat out missed, it means someone

lost concentration. Every man has his key before the start
of a play.–Gordon McCarter

We also all have the responsibility to count the number of players on the field. Just as with the down, the entire crew is punished for too many players on the field. It can happen when there is confusion, especially at the end of the first half or the end of the game, and the offensive team is not sure what it is going to do. This happened in 1981 when the Dallas Cowboys played the Lions in Detroit. The score was tied late in the game. With less than two minutes to go, Detroit forced the Cowboys to punt and moved the ball to the Dallas 30 yard line with 10 seconds left in the game.

The Lions didn't have any more time outs and only two choices–to get their offense set up quickly and throw an incomplete pass to stop the clock and allow time for a field goal attempt, or hope to try the field goal in the last few seconds. The Lions began to do both at the same time with confusion on the offensive team as to which one should be in the game at that time. Players from the field goal unit ran on the field before the regular offensive unit was off. Dallas was having an equally difficult a time trying to decide which defensive unit to have on the field. Detroit kicked a 47-yard field goal to win 27-24. Photographs and video showed the Lions did have 12 men on the field. If there is a penalty on the last play of a half by a defensive team, the down is replayed. But if the offensive team commits the violation, the down is not replayed. Detroit would have been penalized and the game would have gone into overtime.

The Steelers were again the victim of a controversy. Pittsburgh coach Bill Cowher went so far as to confront Referee Gordon McCarter during a game by giving him a photo showing that a penalty for having too many men on the field was unwarranted. The league fined McCarter $4,009 for the erroneous 12th man call.

Calls Most Likely to Be Missed

What are the calls most likely to be missed? Here are my top 10:

1. Offensive holding.
2. False start prior to the snap.
3. Fumble or forward pass by the quarterback.
4. Pass interference.
5. Fumble or not by the ball carrier.
6. Ineligible receiver down field.
7. Whistle before the ball is dead.
8. Running into the kicker (or not).
9. Blocker into the kicker (or not).
10. Encroachment (defense).

The calls most missed are holding. With seven people you can't watch all of the blockers. The umpire, two linesmen and referee are the officials most likely to call holding. Offensive linemen are so skilled today they can hold and not be detected. If there is holding on one side of the line and the play action is on the other side of the line and it was flagrant or gives the team an advantage on that play, the NFL tells us to not call holding. Joe Klecko who played for the Jets and Indianapolis once asked me very nicely, "Fred, what do you call holding?" I said: "Joe, when you win first prize in a rodeo contest, that's holding." He laughed. Basically, that is what the league wanted called at any time. We look for the blockers leading a sweep and those protecting the passer for possible holding. We look for the tight end who can hold his arm out and prevent a defender from moving outside. The interpretation for holding has changed over the years to allow the offensive blockers to extend their arms on pass rushing and blocking has become shoving and shoving has become blocking.

> As much as you know the game, rules come into play. The spirit of the rule on holding is whether or not it places a player at a disadvantage or puts another at an advantage and whether it was of consequence to the play. If you called every holding it would slow the game down.–Jim Tunney

Take for example a situation of a fourth down and a foot to go on the goal line. If the play went straight ahead and the offensive linemen grabbed the defensive linemen just long enough to score or make a first down, then I would call holding. However, if the situation were first down and 10 yards to go and the gain was only a foot or two, I would not call the penalty. This is how sophisticated we had to be to manage the game the way the league wanted it managed. This also is one of the reasons there is confusion when the fans see a television replay on the large screen and think it is holding.

> We could call holding on every play but the league has given us restrictions on when we can make a call. If holding happened, but the player being held didn't have his shirt come out, we may be told to ignore the call. But if the shirt came out, definitely it would be a holding call.–Ben Dreith

Defensive holding in the line doesn't happen nearly as often as offensive holding. It can be critical and normally occurs when an offensive lineman is trying to pull out to lead a running play. The defensive lineman grabs or tackles him to keep him from getting in front of the runner. When this happens it generally is out in the open for everyone to see.

The headlinesman and line judge need to watch the line to see if any player jumps into the neutral zone. Was the ball snapped while he was in the zone? Did a defensive lineman jump into the zone and cause an offensive player to break his stance? Did the offensive lineman break his stance prior to the ball being snapped? Was the offensive tackle and guard lined up with the butt of the center or were they too deep in the backfield? Was it an illegal formation? These are all judgment calls.

> Officials have come under greater scrutiny than ever before with television and replays. Football lends itself to replays because of the break in action and various camera angles. It puts pressure on the officials.–Marv Levy, winningest coach in Buffalo history, directed Bills to four Super Bowls, 21

years as an NFL coach, twice Coach of the Year, elected to
the NFL Pro Football Hall of Fame in January 2001.

On a passing play, did the offensive receiver make contact with the
defensive man such as driving through him and quickly break off to
catch the pass? Or did the defender institute the contact and create a
collision? The defender is not allowed to check or push a receiver beyond
five yards past the line of scrimmage. Was the contact five yards or
beyond? Did the defender hold when the receiver was ready to make a
move? Was the ball in the air when there was contact? Was a pass
thrown on the other side of the field and when the ball is in the air, does
a defender make contact with a receiver on the near side? There is no
foul if the contact happens away from the ball, but was there roughness
and not interference? Was the pass catchable? Were both feet in bounds?
Was the receiver juggling the ball on the sideline? Was the ball caught
or trapped, hitting the ground before a catch? These are all judgment
calls. And the fans are never happy.

> *You need cooperative mechanics on a pass pattern of a*
> *play, shifting the line of vision to lend silent assistance to*
> *the field judge. You need to communicate.*–Gordon
> McCarter

It is very difficult for the umpire on a pass play, especially when a
ball is thrown right over the middle. The mechanic tells the umpire to
turn. The deep officials must look in along with the line judge and head
linesman. Some players will actually use the umpire as an additional
blocker to screen out a defender.

> *The game is really different today. When I played you could*
> *put a hit on a guy. The NFL has changed the rules so much*
> *to favor the offense and uses officiating to protect the*
> *quarterback. Receivers today are quick, fast and with the*
> *reactions of a basketball player. They can shove a defender*
> *with one arm and make a catch with the other. How is the*

official supposed to watch that call?–Sam Huff, NFL Hall of Fame linebacker, consensus All-American and college teammate of Wyant.

Fumble Or Incomplete Pass?

In 1971, my first season as a referee, I thought I had called my last game. The Cowboys were playing the Cardinals in St. Louis. I made five wrong calls in one game. I never had five wrong calls in an entire season, much less all in one game and all for exactly the same call. The quarterback was rushed and as he went back to pass, was hit by a tackler. As he was passing the ball, he lost control of the ball. The question was whether it was a forward pass, an incomplete pass or a fumble. This was strictly a judgment call and I missed the call five times that night.

> *It is almost impossible to work a perfect game. You can't get everything right. Judgment errors are very small in number. On pass interference the officials are constantly making judgment regarding contact. The errors are very, very low.*–Art McNally

This was a problem with mechanics. There are no league guidelines and I had never had a problem before. After this game I changed the way I watched the action. Until that day, every time a quarterback passed, I always watched the quarterback's arm. After that game, I always watched the ball. If the ball was standing still when he was hit, or the ball was moving backwards, I called it a fumble. If the ball was moving forward, it was an incomplete pass. I never missed the same call the rest of my years in the league. Officiating sometimes is learning how to do it right because you did it wrong.

> *Look forward to the challenge of at least one difficult task each day.*–Fred Wyant

Sometimes Participation Backfires

I learned firsthand why Art McNally wanted the referee, and not a committee, to be the decision maker on the field. We had a Chicago Bears-Minnesota Vikings game at Solider Field. It was a beautiful day in Chicago. There was a foul on a punt. When a situation involved rules, I generally deferred to Jerry Bergman, my head linesman, or Dick Hantack, my back judge. They both were very strong in their knowledge of the rules and Jerry was the best in the league. Every member of my crew and our colleagues on other crews had the greatest respect for his knowledge of the rules. I felt the penalty should go one way. The rest of my team looked to Jerry and Dick and felt the call should go the other way. As it turned out, I was right and they were wrong. And in a situation like this, the entire team gets penalized.

> *When the evaluations came back, the entire crew was downgraded. We all thought Bergman and Hantak were right and Fred was wrong. This time he was right. And you never saw a prouder guy, even though he got a ding. He told us that we would have been better off if we had listened to him.*–Bill Quinby.

If You Don't See It How Can You Call It?

In the opening pre-season game one year in Miami, we began our new season with a most unusual incident. The game was between the Eagles and Dolphins. On a pass play, Frank Glover, our headlinesman got tripped on the sidelines and fell down. At that point, the head linesman assumed the responsibility for that side of the field along the sideline from goal to goal. When he fell, Frank could not see whether the receiver was in or out of bounds when the catch was made. Ben Tompkins was my back judge and he was all the way across the field from where the action took place and he couldn't make the call. I had a conference with the crew and decided to call a "no play" and repeat the down.

The call was my responsibility. Eagles coach Dick Vermeil was outside of where he should have been and I got tangled in the headphone wires, tripped and flew in the air. When I landed, I was almost knocked out. Fred came over to ask how I was and whether the pass was complete or incomplete. I told him I didn't know. He then said we'll do it over.–Frank Glover

When Fred ruled 'no play' he went to Dick Vermeil and Don Shula and the team captains and told him what happened and that the down would be replayed. It was the first time I had ever seen it called"–Ben Tompkins

In the Super Bowl one year the officials called a 'no play' and replayed the down. McNally gave us an ultimatum that there will never be a 'no play' again in the NFL. You can imagine what McNally told Fred the next day.–Don Orr

The Good and Bad of Anticipation

Being in the right place at the right time is critical to making the right call. To do this you have to anticipate what is going to happen on a play and when it is going to happen. All of this comes with experience and why I believe it takes five years for an outstanding college official to become an NFL official. The game is different. You have to understand that because it is played professionally at such a high level it is almost hard to comprehend, unless you've been there and experienced it. When rookie officials anticipate it can create problems.

In my rookie year I was working only my second game. It was a pre-season game between the Patriots and Redskins in RFK Stadium in Washington. The offensive team had the ball on the one-yard line. The ball was snapped and the runner had a hole big enough to drive a truck through. As he got near the goal line I signaled touchdown. Then a linebacker came from out of nowhere, hit the runner, the

*ball went in one direction and the running back in another.
I wasn't sure whether it was a touchdown or not, but I had
signaled too soon. I was sick about the call. Pat Summerall
and John Madden severely criticized me on TV. Art McNally
was observing the game and rode with us back to the hotel
after the game. We saw the game again on replay and they
all were constructive and supportive in telling me about my
mistake. I never made that mistake again.*–Joe Haynes

Never Apologize for a Mistake

Cleveland was playing the Steelers in Pittsburgh and the game went
into sudden death overtime. The Browns kicked off. As the Steelers
back began to return the ball, a defender ran into the blocker, shoved
the blocker into the runner and knocked him down. My mind was
going through a process: "If the defender had knocked the runner
down, the ball would be dead at the spot. Instead, he ran into a blocker.
I've never seen this, heard it discussed or read it in the rules. I have a
50/50 chance to getting the play right." I called the ball dead at that
spot. While my mind was computing, the runner got up, ran with the
ball, got hit by a defender, fumbled and Cleveland recovered on the
Pittsburgh 12 yard line. I began waving my arms and brought the ball
back where I originally called it dead and gave it to the Steelers first
down and 10. Terry Bradshaw came in and marched the team 85 yards
to win the game with a touchdown pass.

After the game, Jack Reader, an observer for our game from the
league office, came in our dressing room and asked what I called and
why. He told me I was wrong. I told him in 35 years of officiating it
was the first time I had seen it and had never heard it discussed or read
about such a situation. It still did not excuse my not knowing the rules.
I got abusive phone calls at home from irate Cleveland fans. The league
office told me not to discuss it with the media. On Monday I was in
Pittsburgh for a business meeting. My associate had a businessman
from Cleveland and introduced me as: "This is the guy that #*$&^%
the Browns yesterday." The man didn't even look at me.

I wasn't assigned a Cleveland game for four years. Then I had them in Los Angeles. Sam Rutigliano was still the coach. A play happened in front of the Cleveland bench. The Rams were winning easily but asked for a measurement. Unless a measurement is requested in the last two minutes of a game, you have to honor the request. Sam came over and said: "Ah, for god's sake, Fred, this is ridiculous. We have a plane to catch." I said: "Coach, I'm sorry but by our rules we have to allow them to have the measurement." He mumbled something and as I start to pick up the ball to carry it to the inbounds marker, he began fuming and then exploded. "You @%$*#(& me four years ago in Pittsburgh." He was a nice guy, but obviously the frustration had built in him since that game with the Steelers.

I had a policy of never apologizing to a coach or player because of a call. When I made the call I always thought I was right. Would a coach or player apologize for calling me a #*#*@& or &#*&$^&@ if after seeing the films proved me right? No one play ever resulted in a win or loss. Some are more dramatic based on the timing of the call. But if the game had been perfect, the coaches and players all graded out at 100, then perhaps one play could cost a team the game.

If a player ever called me a name, I would look directly at him and say: "Excuse me" and ask him if he said something. If he repeated it looking me directly in the eyes, I would then throw the flag. If he said: "I wasn't talking to you," I would continue the game and let it go. If it repeated, I would throw him out of the game. You have to know what to hear and what not to hear. There is a tremendous amount of profanity on the field and sidelines. You can never take it personally.

The Inadvertent Whistle

Two rules of the "Ten Commandments" of officiating in the NFL are to blow the whistle only when you see the football and to be great dead ball officials. If you don't see the ball, you don't make the call. I kept the whistle around my neck and in my hand. Many basketball officials keep the whistle in their mouth all the time so they can quickly make a call. It is so easy to get fooled where the ball is and whether or not the ball carrier is down. I want to be sure. I know my brain will tell me if the ball is dead before I can get the whistle to my mouth to stop the play. If a team fumbles the ball and the opposing team recovers, the offensive team keeps possession if the whistle blew before the fumble.

> *Most inadvertent whistles come from over-anticipating. We had a campaign one year and had signs in the dressing rooms, 'Slow Whistle ... So Frustrating.' We took the whistle out of the mouths of several officials and had them wear finger whistles. Then we found that the high percentage of mistakes were being made by those officials who brought the whistles up to their mouths too soon. We junked the idea and let the officials decide how they wanted to wear their whistles.*–Art McNally

During instant replay, the first thing the official in the booth wanted to know is whether or not anyone blew a whistle and, if so, when. This was important if the ball was advanced with the fumble, regardless of who made the recovery. I used to drop my bean bag at the spot the ball carrier fumbled regardless of whether it goes out of bounds or down field. Now if the instant replay official asks if a whistle was blown, I can say "no" but the ball is marked where the ball carrier fumbled it. Correctly officiating a game is a mechanic.

Tom Hensley, my umpire for nine years, had a quick whistle problem one season. This is easy to do when you are in the middle of the line with everyone coming at you. He blew his whistle early two or three times in one game and I told him the following week that if he blew his whistle early in this game, that I was going to personally take the whistle and place it in a part of his anatomy that would require surgery to remove it.

Tom assured me that there would be no problem because he had a new system. Instead of having the whistle on a cord around his neck, he kept it on his fingers. He had turned the whistle away from him and upside down. I thought he would have had to be a contortionist to blow it. We were in Denver and the very first play after the opening kickoff,

I heard the whistle blow when the ball was loose. Tom had his arm twisted in a grotesque way and tooting his whistle. Wrong again! He finally got it all worked out so the problem didn't happen again.

The Immaculate Reception

This is one of the most talked about controversial calls in pro football. On December 23, 1972, Oakland was at Pittsburgh for the AFL championship game. The winner would go to the Super Bowl. I was the alternate official and on the sidelines, in uniform, if needed.

Oakland was leading 7-6. Time was running out. On fourth down with 25 seconds left, Terry Bradshaw threw a desperation pass down field. In the middle of the field, Steelers Frenchey Fuqua and Raider defender Jack Tatum went up for the ball at the same time. It looked like they both touched the ball simultaneously. The ball bounced off one, or both, and out of nowhere, Franco Harris reached down, picked up the ball before it hit the ground and ran all the way for a touchdown and a Steeler victory.

Adrian Burke, who was a field judge for a number of years on my crew, told Fred Swearington, the referee, that the ball was last touched by Tatum, making it legal for Harris to catch and advance the ball. No film, video or photograph has showed clearly what happened. The rules then said that if two people on the offensive team touched the ball, it was an incomplete pass. If the defense touched it first, or in between, then was all right for any offensive player to catch the ball.

The officials met for a conference and after two or three minutes it seemed like forever. By this time hundreds of Pittsburgh fans had run from the stands on to the ends and sides of the field. My concern was that the crew might be confused over the rule. I saw Fred Wyant in his white jacket standing on the back of the end line and decided I needed to talk to him to get him to communicate with Fred Swearington. I asked Joe Gordon, then the Steelers public relations man, to ask his contact on the field to get Fred

Wyant on the line for me, and specifically told him he was the alternate and in a white jacket and where he was standing.–Art McNally

Jim Boston, who ran security and was in control of the playing field area, went over to Fred Swearington during his conference and asked his if he wanted to talk to anyone upstairs, and if so, he would show him where the phone was in the dugout. Swearington then went to the phone to call McNally.–Daniel M. Rooney, president, Pittsburgh Steelers

I saw Fred Swearington go into the dugout and use the telephone. When he hung up, he came back on the field he signaled "Touchdown." Most people, and especially Raiders owner Al Davis and coach John Madden were absolutely furious and thought that Art McNally made the call in the press box. I always wonder what would have happened if Fred came out and signaled "incomplete pass." Adrian Burke made the key call.

That play led to the NFL changing the rule in 1978 to legalize the double touch.

I had hardly sat down in my seat when I was told, Fred is on the line for you. But it was the wrong Fred. The person on the field didn't listen or else got very mixed up. Fred Swearington, the referee, had left the field to take the call. This was a first in the league. The first thing he said was 'two of my men rule the ball was touched by a defensive player.' I told him 'fine, OK' and nothing more. He never asked my opinion regarding the play. He hung up, walked back on the field, faced the press box and signaled touchdown. I was concerned how this might look.–Art McNally

There was no instant replay in those days but it would have confirmed what the officials said. If you have any understanding of forces or are a physics major you would

understand." Chuck Noll, the only coach to win four Super Bowls, Pittsburgh Steeler coach from 1969-1991, Pro Football Hall of Fame, NFL coach for 23 years.

The Unwritten and Unspoken Rule

There was one cardinal rule we all followed that was handed down from one generation of officials to another generation. We called it "time and score." In the National Basketball Association it could best be described as "no harm, no foul." Look at the game action in the closing minutes of a professional basketball game–if one team is being blown out, you'll see fouls overlooked that would have been called earlier in the game. The officials in the National Hockey League also appear to disregard calls in the closing minutes unless the outcome of the game can be changed.

Our unwritten and unspoken rule in the NFL was that in the closing minutes of a game, if a team was being beaten and had no chance of winning, penalties that had no bearing on the outcome of the game– whether a team would win or lose–should be ignored.

With 10 seconds left in the game and a team was losing say 31-6, and someone is offsides, we didn't make the call. During my early years in the league, at the two-minute warning, the veterans on the crew would say "Keep the flag deep in your pocket." The exception was anything flagrant like a personal foul. Holding, offsides, encroachment and other similar penalties would be ignored.

For obvious reasons, you won't find this "rule" in writing anywhere. It also was never discussed at any clinic or league meeting. But we all understood very clearly that this was league policy and was what the league wanted.

This all changed in 1979 when Dale Hamer and Bama Glass were officiating a game between the Green Bay Packers and the Houston Oilers. Dale was the head linesman and Bama was the line judge, opposite each other on the line of scrimmage. Houston was winning 10-0 and the clock showed only four seconds left in the game.

Glenn Dickey was the Green Bay quarterback and Bart Starr the team's coach. There was absolutely no way Green Bay could overcome a 10-0 deficit in four seconds. On the last play of the game, Dickey dropped back to pass, fumbled the ball, and a Houston player picked it up and ran it into the end zone for a touchdown. The score was now 16-0 and time had run out.

The next thing I heard was that Dale and Bama had been suspended.

After he was told about his suspension, that Tuesday evening Bama had an emergency appendectomy. For whatever reason he would not have been able to work any more that season. Dale was assigned a playoff game. Bama recovered quickly and was assigned to the crew of the Pro Bowl in February. When the story got out, Bart Starr felt the penalty was too severe and was upset about Dale and Bama being suspended. He called Art to ask him to reconsider saying he didn't believe what happened was serious enough for a suspension.

> *Fred decided to be the spokesman for all of the officials said we should be paid for the game we were suspended or the officials should refuse to work the playoffs. He called for a strike. I didn't like being fined, but I was wrong and didn't want it to turn out like this. I felt we all should just forget it, but Fred was adamant.*–Dale Hamer

The league brought all of the officials working playoffs together for a meeting in Pittsburgh. As we were all sitting there waiting for the meeting to begin. Nothing was said about the suspension. So, I got up and blasted McNally and the entire system, saying Dale and Bama were only doing what the rest of us were doing by following the unwritten, unspoken, league policy.

With expansion teams and new divisions and conferences came complicated formulas how teams make playoffs. Points scored became one of the tie-breakers, so a "missed" call might have a bearing. But if you go back and review all of the tie-breaker situations for teams making playoffs this probably never became a factor. The only people who might be angry would be the gamblers if this upset the "line" on the game. I couldn't care less about the point spread and no official I ever knew did either.

More Controversy With the Steelers

Donnie Orr, my field judge, was the only person on the spot to make a difficult call in a Pittsburgh-Houston game. Jack Renfro caught the ball in the end zone and the question was whether or not it was touchdown. Donnie said Renfro juggled the ball in bounds and did not have control of the ball as he went out of the end zone. The touchdown was taken away from the Steelers. Television looked at it from six different angles and even the media couldn't agree. It was too close to call. Either team would have claimed robbery regardless of his decision. Donnie later told me: "Fred, there is no play too close to call. Even if you are the only person there, you still have to make the call." On any call, especially a touchdown, you have to be absolutely sure it is a score.

Some calls are missed because of lack of experience.–Jerry Bergman

I had another experience when I was moved back to line judge. I had a game in Miami the weekend before the Dolphins were to play in Buffalo for the conference championship. In the first half, Miami had the ball first down and goal to go on the one yard line. Four times the Dolphins ran the ball into my side of the line and did not once score. As we were going off the field for halftime, Don Shula, the Miami coach, storms me and yells: "How in @#^$&* could that not be a touchdown?" I replied: "You only wish that you had me on the goal in Buffalo next week and the Bills have four shots at your defense. He looked and me and scowled: "Ah, *#*$& you."

I didn't see the ball, so I didn't make the call. Was there a score? I don't think so. Could there have been? Possibly.

Heads or Tails?

Anyone who followed the NFL during the 1998 season will remember the controversial coin toss on Thanksgiving Day when Pittsburgh and Detroit went into overtime. As the visiting team, the Steelers Jerome Bettis made the call while the coin was in the air. Referee Phil Luckett said Bettis called "heads-tails" so he went with the first thing he heard, "heads." The coin came up tails and Luckett declared that Detroit won the toss. Teammate Carnell Lake was standing next to Bettis and says he tried to tell Luckett he was wrong. The Lions elected to receive and took the kickoff, went 41 yards down the field in seven plays and kicked a 42-yard field goal to win the game. This incident became one of the biggest controversies of the season. Under NFL rules, Luckett could have re-tossed the coin if he felt there were sufficient grounds. Now the league has three officials at the coin toss. One is with each team and the visiting team captain must call "heads" or "tails" before the coin toss.

I had a similar problem, but not as controversial, in one of my first games as a referee. New Orleans was playing at Buffalo and both captains were former West Virginia Mountaineers–Bobby Gresham of the Saints and Jimmy Braxton of the Bills. Gresham, as the visiting captain, called and said "heads." The coin landed "tails" and I mistakenly said, "Bobby, you win the coin toss." Braxton and the Bills players protested that I was wrong. I couldn't help overhear an older, seasoned veteran official who was part of my team tell another official, "What kind of a game is this going to be when he #%*@! the coin toss?" I did get it right in the end.

I had another experience with Chicago at Denver. Dick Butkus, the Bears' captain called "tails." It landed heads, and he immediately yelled: "I called heads." I told him three times that he had called tails. He again said: "I called heads." And I again replied, "Dick, you called tails." At that point he said, "Toss it again." We all laughed.

CHAPTER IV

The Influence of Television

Until the television networks began to flex their muscle and truly take NFL football into the realm of entertainment, officials were virtually anonymous. The league liked it that way. So did we.

The seven of us on the field are already highly visible in our zebra-striped black and white shirts and white knickers. No one is more visible than the referee when the television camera zooms in as he explains the call, penalty or decision. Most players don't get that kind of exposure during a game.

Once television wired for us sound, some of my fellow referees even developed personality traits and mannerisms, such as Red Cashion and the way he used to yell: "Firrrrrrrst Down!" Now people know who we are. They remember that Jerry Markbreit was the referee in their home team's game last week. Or that Jim Tunney made that controversial call three weeks ago.

The late Tommy Bell, one of the league's all-time great referees, even was selected by a couple of sponsors to do television commercials that were aired during a Super Bowl. There are only 16 referees in the NFL and each one is on television 20 times each season. I don't think the officials on Park Avenue were very happy when Bell started doing commercials. In those days they preferred us to just be anonymous.

Until television wired the referee for sound, officiating was always non-verbal communications. It bothered us a lot when we were told we had to turn on the mike, step into the camera position, announce the penalty and give the signal. Some referees were confused and pointed in the wrong direction, gave a wrong verbal description, sometimes even the wrong signal, and everything was very confusing. I never liked it. It was like a school teacher identifying you in front of all of the others in the classroom.– Jim Tunney

The first time I really had a feeling for how much television influenced the NFL was when McNally and Val Pinchbeck, Jr., the league's senior vice president-broadcasting and network television, met with all of the referees over lunch during one of our pre-season clinics. At that time we discussed the new television guidelines for games during the season. We were told how long halftime would be and many time outs would be allowed per quarter, such as five in the first and four in each of the following quarters.

With the new television contract, there are five television timeouts in each quarter for a total of 20. The networks have to get their rights fees back someway and the most obvious is from sponsors. They can raise the commercial prices only so much but it is easier just to add more commercials, making the game even longer. The breaks are 1 minute and 50 seconds and the referee starts the play clock 1 minute and 50 seconds after he signals a timeout. Pinchbeck emphasized the importance of having my line judge go to the television truck as soon as we arrived at the football field to get the correct time. The "correct time" was whatever the television network told us.

TV controls the game. They tell us what to do, when to start, when to stop. But when it lines the owners pockets with gold, they don't care.–Jerry Bergman.

We were told to tell the television production people, in a meeting in our dressing room, exactly how the game would be run. The kickoff time was always predetermined by the league but also was subject to change by the network. Club management can ask the referee to delay the start of a game up to five minutes for the benefit of television and radio fans who otherwise might receive an incomplete broadcast.

Television completely changed the tempo of one of my games. The football game was pre-empted by coverage of Pope John Paul II's visit to the United States. As a result, we had no timeouts at all during the first half for television commercials. So it wouldn't lose any income, the network insisted on making up the eight or nine commercials it missed by news coverage of the Pope during the second half.

> *Whether it is the first game you're officiating or your last, there is always extra pressure on us when we have a Monday night football game. America is watching. We are the only game in town. All of the coaches, players and my officiating peers are tuned in. You can't make a mistake because if you do, you not only embarrass yourself, you embarrass the entire league as a representative of all of the officials.*–Bill Carrollo

Today television can have whatever it wants. In 1998, CBS, ABC and Fox television paid $17.6 billion for the rights to NFL games for eight years, even though analysts project this will leave each network with a huge financial loss. Television pays the salaries of the players and management and provides the owners with a handsome profit.

> *Television made the game. Pete Rozelle knew television and what it could do. He worked hand-in-hand with the networks to make the game so great and so popular. Pete understood our problems. If we asked for something and he said "no" it was because it wasn't good for the game. We asked for a lot of things and got them because he allowed us to have a certain free rein. When you're working with a Pete*

Rozelle you are stimulated to do better things. That's how innovations came along.–Hal Uplinger

The Man on the Sidelines

Some people might think I spent as much time watching the television coordinator on the sidelines as I did the players on the field. The referee has to be alert for a signal from the television coordinator who will request a timeout "at the next opportunity" by stepping to the edge of the field with arms crossed over the chest. Some wore orange jackets or vests so they were very conspicuous. I would acknowledge that I saw his time out request by pointing to the ground. We would always meet before the game to get acquainted and go over procedures.

When you know who you are, you don't have to tell anybody else.–Fred Wyant

When I called time out I would wave it on the field and then point to the coordinator on the sideline. The coordinator would acknowledge by stepping on the field and putting his right arm with a closed fist over his left shoulder.

I would stand beside the television coordinator five minutes before the game until I was told that it was all right for the other officials to bring the team captains to the center of the field. He then would tell me to go out for the coin toss.

Television timeouts were generally slotted following the change of possession such as the return of a kick, recovery of a fumble or a pass interception, so long as it did not result in the defensive team returning the ball inside the opponent's 40-yard line. At the conclusion of the down I would reconfirm the television break by signaling time. The referee and the referee alone is the only person who can decide whether or not and when a television time out is to be granted.

If a player was injured and a time out called and I felt there would be a reasonable delay because of the injury, it was my job to check with the television coordinator to see whether or not television wanted to go to a commercial.

The back judge and I needed to be aware of the number of time outs television needs to fulfill its commitments to the sponsors. This is important so that no television time out will interfere with a team's momentum. As a policy, we were not to call the first time out until both teams had possession of the ball. This would change, of course, if one team took the opening kickoff and kept the ball for 10 minutes marching the length of the field. When all was said and done, whatever television wanted, it got. Whenever I personally tried to take charge of what was happening in a game, if it conflicted with the wishes of the network, I caught #*&%*& from the league office.

In addition to the television coordinator, I also was expected to cooperate with the public address announcer and in communicating information to press box if questions came up regarding certain penalties or calls. I was expected to know the location of the television booth, radio announcer and press before the start of any game.

> *We had a Monday night game in Denver and were clowning in the dressing room before going out on the field when there was a pounding on our door. Fred had his microphone turned on and all of our discussion was being heard by everyone in Mile High Stadium.*–Wilson Gosier

Some network TV coordinators could be rather officious at times. The ABC team for Monday night games had different procedures from the other networks. I had a Monday night game once in Miami and the coordinator made everything a major event. The person in charge of my microphone came into our dressing room in a panic because he thought the remote microphone transmitter box that I wore on my belt was broken. He said he didn't know what he was going to do. I told him: "Don't worry. I'll take care of everything." I asked him to please let me see the box. He extended his hand and I put mine on top of his and the box and yelled: "Heal! Heal!" Everyone laughed and my crew was at ease before the started the game. And the microphone even worked!

HENR

The league always sent a vice president or assistant vice president from the executive office to Monday night games. They were in the dressing room watching all of this and walked out without a word. I'm sure McNally got an earful the next day.

> You would have thought Fred was an evangelist preacher the way he shouted out 'heal.' He did keep us loose.–Don Orr

I've heard complaints about me from some television producers and announcers who said I'm difficult to work with. While I may have taken a number of liberties with league policies off the field, once I was on the field I enforced the rules and regulations by the book. I would always add a few seconds more just for the transition before I blew my whistle for the teams to huddle before resuming play. But to delay a game a minute or two, no.

> In 1974 I worked NBA basketball on CBS with Pat Summerall. He also did NFL football and knowing we were both from West Virginia, Pat told me that Fred, as a referee, was very difficult to work with. He didn't cut any slack for television if they were running over their time. This is a compliment to Fred as a no-nonsense official. The officials in the NBA are lenient and very cooperative with broadcasters.–Hot Rod Hundley, basketball All-American at West Virginia University, NBA All-Star with the Los Angeles Lakers and television and radio announcer for the Utah Jazz.
>
> If there is action on the field when a TV commercial has ended, this is the fault of the producer and director. Don't blame Fred Wyant or any referee for this. The referee starts his watch when he signals the coordinator on the sidelines. Too often an announcer wants to keep talking another 20 or 30 seconds about a play so the program is

already late going into the commercial. When time is up, play starts whether or not television is ready.–Hal Uplinger

Two minutes for a television time out can feel like an hour on a cold, blustery day in Soldier Field in Chicago with the wind chill coming off Lake Michigan. There isn't much the seven of us on the field or the thousands in the stands can do except wait. It is ironic that more time is committed to television commercials–more than 36 minutes–when there are only 13 minutes of actual play action during a game. Each team also gets three timeouts per half, or a total of 12 timeouts during the game. Television can also use these for commercials. The 12 timeouts represent more time than actual minutes of game action.

Year-in-and-year-out, Fred would always have the fastest football games. He would get the football and put it in play and kept the gave moving faster than any other referee.–Jack Fette

The Affect On Young Officials

An official has to work hard to mentally prepare himself to handle the negatives that can be created by the image projected by television replays and especially on the large screen Jumbotrons in many stadiums. One of the toughest things for a new official to deal with is being unfortunate enough to miss a call early in a game and early in the season. New officials must understand that this is part of the game and that we're going to work to correct those mistakes by sharing and discussing with them how they might have better judgment.

The more you do for other people, the better you feel about yourself.–Fred Wyant
The Jumbotron did intimidate some officials. It could make you look bad in front of fans. But when I go on the field I'm doing my job and if a replay shows something else,

so be it. Fans and coaches and players always see it different.—Jim Tunney

Even spectators today want to see a replay of any controversial play to they can judge for themselves whether a pass had been caught, whether the receiver was in bounds or out of bounds, and whether they thought the official's call was correct. They then share their pleasure or displeasure with those on the field.

> *With Jumbotrons the hometown fans get to see a play two, three or four times and interpret it as they want it to be and not as it is. The replay screen in the stadium does not tell the story and is subject to the fan's interpretation. They see things as they want them to be and not as they are.*—Gordon McCarter
>
> *If you can't stand pressure, you're in the wrong business being an official. Pressure is one of the appealing things I like about being in the business.*—Ben Tompkins

The large television screens never bothered me. I never looked them and told my crew not to look up. It may even be a league policy today. While older, experienced officials would not be troubled by questioning whether or not the right call had been made, seeing the screen, as blurry as it was and with camera angles that really don't tell the true story, it could be devastating for a rookie. This does made an official's job more difficult than it needs to be.

> *Never look up to see what is on TV. Don't second guess yourself, regardless how bad you want to see the play again. The league gives us satellite dishes so we can tape our games and see them as soon as we get home. If you were involved in a controversial call, remember it as you called it, not how you saw it on television.*—Dale Hamer
>
> *The only time I really felt pressure from television was before a Rams-Giants game in Yankee Stadium. I was stand-*

ing there singing the National Anthem and the television
camera was on me. I'm in the airline business and the next
day I had calls from friends all over the world who told me
that at least I knew the words."–Jack Steffen

There are individuals with the network officials and commentators,
team owners, coaches and even players who believe that when an official
makes a mistake or misses a call because there were not 14 replays to
look at, then that official should be suspended, fined or even fired, on
the spot. Let me assure you that it takes time to develop an NFL
official. I never heard of any television announcer being fined, fired or
suspended for mispronouncing a name or misidentifying a player. Or
an owner for making a wrong draft choice? Or coaches or players for
their mistakes?

Television has been one of the best things that has happened
to officials. Instant replay shows the credibility of the
officials.–Red Cashion

Because of the influence of television there has been a cry by different
groups to have full time officials. Major League Baseball and the National
Basketball Association have full time officials paid year-round. But what
type of person would the league get for professional football if five days
a week someone had to spend watching films of calls and plays,
practicing with certain teams, and taking course work so you were
perfect as far as the rules were concerned. With all of that the official
still has to understand the game which comes only from experience of
officiating. The official still has to make judgment calls on almost every
play. And as instant replay proved, the officials in the NFL are right
more than 99 percent of the time.

I always thought NFL officials should be full-time. The
coaches work all year long, the players work out all year
long to better themselves and the officials are the only part
of professional football that is part time.–Kellen Winslow

At every game there were observers and league office officials who are in our dressing room immediately after a game if the television replays showed a bad call. They were quick to let our crew know we had missed a call. This creates an undue negative condition for younger officials. Young officials need constant praise to help develop their officiating skills. I never refereed a game that I couldn't tell my crew afterwards that they had done a great job individually and as a team. When the league sent us the video it appeared that more emphasis was placed on how wrong the game was being officiated rather than how right it was officiated.

I differed with those sitting in the Park Avenue suites and their management and leadership philosophy. I really didn't care what the league office thought about the crew if we only missed a couple of things. We weren't interested in what our supervisors had to say or learn from what they had to say. As the referee, if I thought they were picky with their evaluation, I wouldn't stand by and let someone feel like they were destroyed as far as their officiating career was concerned. Careers have gone down the tube when officials made too many bad judgment calls and couldn't understand the difference between a real call and a phantom call, but these were few and far between.

Are the officials perfect? No. In my opinion, they are the most perfect or closest to being perfect in all of the elements that makes an NFL football game, including even television.

CHAPTER V

The Not-So-Instant Replay

From 1986 through the 1991 season the seven of us on the field had another man on our team–the instant replay official who sat in the press box and reviewed television videotape on controversial calls. The big problem was that instant replay wasn't instant. It took too long to get an answer and even then our instant replay official was vulnerable to making a mistake. Our team member in the press box, who was a retired official, was graded according to his accuracy the same as we were on the field.

During the 1998 football season there was probably more controversy involving calls made by football officials that ever before. And not just in the NFL, but in colleges as well. And, the complaints have continued to increase. Television doesn't miss much. Now there are so many cameras covering the games and with modern technology, the viewer can virtually be right on top of the ball, often when an official cannot. The television commentators are always quick to point out mistakes made by officials and replay and replay again any controversial plays. Mistakes by officials became the favorite subject for many sports commentators and columnists. Fans began demanding instant replay.

One of the most talked about controversies during the 1998 season was the Pittsburgh-Detroit coin toss before the overtime. Some critics blame the referee for the Steelers' loss. The media felt there were significant errors in other games that could have been corrected by instant replay. One was television showing Jets' quarterback Vinny Testaverde short of the goal line when he was awarded a touchdown that might have knocked Seattle out of the playoffs. Advocates who want instant replay also use the following examples to support their case:

* The 1995 AFC championship game when Kordell Stewart of Pittsburgh caught a five-yard touchdown pass as an ineligible receiver after stepping over the end line. The Colts lost the game 20-16 and a trip to Super Bowl XXX.
* There were several in 1997 that affected playoffs. Detroit Lions cornerback Bryant Westbook was lying with his upper body out of bounds when he intercepted a pass against the New York Jets. And Kansas City tight end Tony Gonzalez was ruled out of bounds when he made a catch against Denver while video showed he was inbounds. The Broncos went on to win.

A replay would have shown that Eagles defensive end Mike Mamula tipped Troy Aikman's fourth-down pass at the line of scrimmage making contact by cornerback Charles Dimry legal. Instead, pass interference was ruled and the Cowboys drive led to a game winning touchdown.

Instant replay is back. Today's version combines elements of the one we used with a coaches' challenge system that was experimented with in the 1998 preseason. When the league discontinued instant replay following the 1991 season, the subject was discussed at almost every annual league meeting.

To be reinstated, instant replay needed votes from 24 of the 31 owners. Until the March 1999 meeting, when the ballots were counted the "yes" votes were always two to three short.

> Instant replay has no place in football. No one can make the game errors free. It just adds another potential for error. It destroys the momentum of the game and for that reason alone it should be ruled out. Numerous mistakes were made by the replay official who had to rely solely on the videotape

given by the network We never had enough qualified instant replay reviewers. I hope it never returns to the game.–Ben Tompkins

The first actual use of instant replay was in the former U. S. Football League during the 1985 season. While instant replay had been under study for several years at the NFL, the USFL, which played its games in the spring, gets credit for the innovation. The system the USFL used was a coaches' challenge system. Each coach was allowed two challenges each half and given red flags to throw to have a call reviewed. Cal Lepore was head of officiating for the USFL and was responsible for helping Commissioner Harry Usher introduce his approach to instant replay. Lepore later became a referee in the NFL.

Tex Schramm, president of the Dallas Cowboys and chairman of the league's Competition Committee, was well known for his love of technology and was responsible for adapting instant replay for the NFL.

When I became commissioner of the USFL in January 1985, the league was in a financial mess. We were looking for something to make a splash with television and our contracts with ABC and ESPN, so we tried instant replay during the exhibition season and continued for the rest of the season. Our system did not hold up the game. It became part of a coaching thing because coaches were limited to two challenges each half. In all, coaches threw 45 red flags and 20 calls were overturned. Under pressure from the USFL, instant replay was adopted by the NFL. They made the mistake of having every play subject to recall.–Harry Usher, former USFL commissioner and executive vice president of the 1984 Los Angeles Olympic Organizing Committee.

During the six years of instant replay, the league found that there was no increase in the number of correct or incorrect calls made because of television. There was no significant difference in the level of officiating.

We still were right 99 percent of the time. Certainly there were times when a controversial call was changed and corrected. But there were other times the replay official missed the call and made the wrong decision.

> *I did not care for instant replay. It slowed the pace of the game. It detracted from the officials on the field running the game.*–Robert Moore

According to the NFL, during the 1998 season, in reviews of every play from every game by the league's officiating department, only 77 out of a possible 37,060 plays were deemed reversible–a percentage of .002.

> *During the first year of instant replay there were more than 40,000 plays in all of the games and we reversed less than 40 calls. That's a record of 0.001! It was misunderstood as an aid to officiating and not an end all.*–Art Holst

People thought that the networks had television cameras in every conceivable nook and cranny so they couldn't miss anything. The networks didn't have cameras in all places. They found out that it was impossible or too expensive to do. If they bring back instant replay sometime in the future, with the new technology using mini cameras, probably they can add many more cameras in new locations–even from the goal posts. There still were many times when the instant replay didn't show the play clearly or from the proper angle for the replay official to make a decision.

> *It is 10 times harder doing instant replay than being on the field. I liked it because the objective is to get back to the locker room after the game being as close to perfection as you can possibly get, whether it is from a fellow official helping you out on a ruling or by a replay official. Sooner or later someone will look at the tape and know whether you*

are right or wrong. Replay was put into get the big, important plays. Had we used it that way we still would have it.–Fritz Graf, NFL field judge and instant replay official for 24 years

The plays we reviewed were to determine if a pass was complete, incomplete or intercepted and in the field of play at a sideline or end line. If the receiver or defensive back, in the case of an interception, was forced out of bounds and so designated by the covering official, instant replay was not involved. The system wanted to determine if there was a fumble or was the runner down by contact prior to fumbling. If the covering official ruled the runner was down and blew his whistle, instant replay did not get involved.

Instant replay slows the game. With seven officials on the field, unless one is really fooled on a play or out of position, there is no reason a call will be missed.–Fred Heichmer

Instant replay was to determine if there was a question whether a pass was forward or backward and on an attempted forward pass when the quarterback was hit was it a forward pass or a fumble. It also was to check the ball breaking the plane of the goal line in player possession, adjustment of the ball when a first down was involved, plays involving touching of the football and if more than 11 men were on the field.

Instant replay proved the official right on one of the all-time great calls. It was a wet, rainy night and the receivers had towels in their belts to keep wiping their hands dry. The receiver made a great catch with both feet in bounds, but the official called the pass incomplete. The towel becomes part of the uniform and any part of the uniform that is out of bounds before the pass is caught with both feet in bounds makes the catch an incomplete pass. This is what the official called. Instant replay ran very slowly showed the towel from the belt hitting the ground before both feet touched in bounds. Unfortunately, the television announcers didn't know the rules and kept arguing that the call should have been reversed. Too bad, because the public was misled when the officials should have been praised.–Art Holst

Instant replay was a momentum breaker. It was most obvious for the teams on the field, but it also became a momentum breaker for the officiating crews who work hard to get into the flow of the game. You are all moving together and then everything comes to a complete stop and you wait. Then you get a decision and have to jump back into the game.

The timing factor was abnormal to the game. It took too long, was too technical, broke concentration and some officials didn't like it. It was designed to correct obvious errors and used to call balls and strikes.–Dale

What became difficult was when our team member in the press box would reverse the call of an official on the field who had made a tough, judgment call. The man on the field is being told he made the wrong call without having the opportunity to see the tape or participate in the decision. This did not cause happy times on the field for a crew. I don't think that the average fan knew that the instant replay official was part of our team. He had a microphone wired to the umpire who could stop the game any time to look at a play. He would be with us in our meetings and discuss his mechanics and our mechanics working with him. Still, those of us on the field didn't like what his job was professionally.

My objection to instant replay was that it interfered with the game.–Red Cashion

Instant replay has its place, but as an official, I think the game belongs to the fans, officials, coaches and players, and that's it. You can't replay every little controversial play that

comes up. Coaches make mistakes. Players make mistakes.
Don't single out one agency.–Mike Lisetski

I had a lot of games in Miami. Most of them involved some sort of controversy with Don Shula in the center of the storm. Instant replay took over one call when there was a disagreement between Jerry Bergman, my head linesman, and Bill Carrollo, in his rookie year as a side judge. The Dolphins were in a two-minute drill and on a pass play, Bergman called the play complete and Carrollo called it incomplete. As I walked over for a conference with the two, Bill tells me: "I have out of bounds and Berggie has inbounds." Berggie turns to me and says: "Let the kid have it." I signal incomplete pass. During this time, Shula is on the sidelines and is ready to explode.

The call goes to instant replay. Shula figured the call would be overturned and ruled a completed pass for Miami. The ruling came back that the play stands as called. By this time Shula was ballistic.

> *Shula couldn't believe Wyant would support me, a rookie,*
> *over an experienced, senior official like Bergman. was lucky.*
> *My first thought was that Berggie let me have the call*
> *knowing he would be right on the replay. But the decision*
> *came back in my favor. I really believe the instant replay*
> *could have gone either way. This was great support*
> *mechanism for me in my first year in the league. And I*
> *earned respect from Don Shula. When I had a senior referee*
> *like Fred it made my start very special.*–Bill Carrollo
>
> *Instant replay put more pressure on rookies and*
> *younger officials. They didn't know what to call.*–Ben Dreith

The worst part of instant replay was when the replay official said it was inconclusive. We had been waiting for an answer and he couldn't make a decision one way or the other. It was especially difficult on those winter days when the wind chill was zero or below. Sometimes the players just didn't understand why it was taking so long. It just created confusion. You can imagine the frustration it caused the fans in the stands. This also would have been an opportunity to let television take a time out, but we never knew how quickly we would hear from the press box.

> *I was an instant replay official for four years and hope it doesn't come back under any circumstance. The officials do a fine job on the field. They make so few mistakes. Replay is elaborated on because of media attention. Often we didn't get to see the shots we needed to see.*–Jack Fette

One time a veteran official came to me while the tapes were being reviewed and said: "If they stop this game one more time, I'm walking off the field." I tried to calm him down and said: "It's part of the rule if you want to be an official. Rules are rules and we have to follow them." Whether or not he would have walked off, I don't know. But knowing him the way I do, the odds would have been 50/50. The following week in our meeting I told our crew that we just mentally had to recognize this is going to happen and we need to support each other and help each other so instantly when the decision is made we can get back into the flow of our game. Otherwise, we were in danger of having an outside element control the way we were handling the game.

> *Instant replay sucks. In 30 years in the league I never once dropped a pass in the end zone, fumbled the ball on the goal line and never put 12 men on the field. Why should we be the only ones not permitted to make a mistake?*–Jerry Bergman

Communications was a problem during the first year. John Keck tells the story of an Oakland-Kansas City game when a ruling from the instant replay official didn't work. John was the umpire and the one wired to the press box and the instant replay official. Oakland threw a pass in the end zone and there was controversy whether or not the receiver was in or out of bounds. The play went to instant replay. "Jack

Reeder was in the press box and all I could hear him say was 'plete',"
Keck told me. "I asked him to repeat what he said and all I could hear
out of the walkie-talkie-type equipment was 'plete'. I assumed he was
saying 'complete' and told my referee to signal touchdown. The extra
point was kicked, Oakland has 7 points on the scoreboard and then we
heard Reeder was trying to tell us 'incomplete.' By that time, the points
stood."

*In a Monday conference call with McNally and Reeder, we
decided that was the time to not only change the equipment,
but the terminology. We would say either 'reversal' to change
the call, or 'continue play' if we thought the call on the field
was right. And the instant replay official would repeat this
three times to the umpire.–John Keck*

*You were given very specific instructions as to what
you could say regarding instant replay. We were supposed
to say "After further review by the replay official, the play
stands," or "is reversed" with the emphasis on the person
in the press box. Following a disagreement by two of my
officials in the end zone in Chicago over whether the play
was a touchback or a safety, I made the decision. It went to
the replay official and came back that I was right. Since we
made the right decision on the field, I announced that the
play stands and did not precede it by "after further review"
or mention the "replay official" and I was criticized by the
league office for doing this. They wanted to emphasize the
involvement of the man in the box.–Ben Dreith*

It is obvious that it is the owner's game. They make the rules and the
players and officials just play by the rules given them. You also do the
best job you possibly can based on the fact that you are the most elite
officiating group in professional sport.

*I was never in favor of instant replay, although Tex Schramm
(president and general manager of the Cowboys) favored it.*

*He also was on the NFL's competition committee. I thought
it tied up the game too much and hurt the game. You have
to keep people from using it too much. The new system
being tried this year might cut down the challenges. You
have to curtail the coaches from using it every time they
want to challenge a call.*–Tom Landry, Dallas Cowboys coach
for 28 years, had 20 consecutive winning seasons, Pro
Football Hall of Fame, perfected the flex defense and shotgun
offense.

*I liked instant replay. When you walked off the field
you knew there was no question about the call. The bad
point was it made younger officials more hesitant to make
a critical call because you got downgraded if you were overruled.*–Don Orr

I could virtually tell you from year-to-year how the owners would vote
on instant replay. It all depends on which team got gored the year
before. Many owners have switched back and forth being advocates or
adversaries of instant replay.

*You really don't realize the full impact of instant replay or
television until after you are away from the game. Then you
realize the magnitude of the decision being made.*–Chuck
McCallum

The only way to solve the problem is to come up with a format that
satisfies everybody. Then a decision must be made whether to look at
the replay with no penalty if the official is overruled, or to penalize the
team if the game was stopped and the official was right.

*Instant replay should be used only in certain situations.
Make the coach use it as a tool for one or two plays a game
and for important game-deciding plays.*–Kellen Winslow
*I have no strong feelings one way or the other about instant
replay. What it did was pin point exactly how good a job*

we on-the-field officials are doing. If it can help us get a play correct and it doesn't cost anyone a game, then it's an important tool.–Dick Hantack

A Replay for Replay in 1998

Instant replay came back for pre-season games during the 1998 season and was officially adopted for league play in 1999. In 1997, 10 teams voted against instant replay and nine did in 1998. By 1999, only Arizona, Cincinnati and the New York Jets opposed the system. The league first experimented with its new concept during 10 nationally televised pre-season games and fine tuned it for official play. With the new system, the referee reviewed only calls challenged by one of the head coaches. Like the USFL plan, a coach was given two challenges a game with the opportunity to ask for a review tied to his team's time outs.

During the final two minutes of each half and during any overtime period, the review can be initiated by a replay official in the press box. This replay official can ask for any many plays to be reviewed as he thinks necessary. Neither team is charged for a timeout for a press box-initiated review. Any other time, if the play stands as called, the coach is charged with a timeout. Also, a challenge can be made and recognized even if a team has used all of its timeouts.

All of the replay reviews are now conducted by the referee using a field-level monitor after talking with other officials involved with the play. The decision is reversed only when the referee has indisputable visual evidence that the call should be changed. All reviews are limited to 90 seconds. Timing begins when the referee begins his review inside the box, or looking at the field-level monitor.

Some owners objected to the proposal because they believed it placed another burden on coaches and gave fans the media another opportunity to second-guess them. Other teams are philosophically opposed to any kind of replay while others favor any kind of replay system.

I'm not a big proponent of instant replay. The new system being experimented with is terrible. It put too much pressure on the coaches. They have enough to do.–Daniel Rooney

For the first time, the final decision was made by the officials on the field and not by an official in the press box without any input from the referee and his crew. Television monitors are placed on the sidelines at each 20-yard line. I can't tell you how many times I wish I had a monitor on the field during times a play was being reviewed in the press box.

A simple new hand held television monitor is now available from Scanz Communications. It was developed by Tony Verna, who, with Hal Uplinger, brought instant replay, the isolated camera and slow motion to television sports. According to Sheldon A. Saltman, president of the company, the Scanz Scannor weighs only 12 ounces and is about the size of a pack of cigarettes. It receives a radio signal feed of the game and stores the last play in memory. It can record up to 30 minutes of video footage. The official can play, freeze, advance frame by frame, or fast forward to the next angle of the play and can review a play in 15 seconds. The system has been tried unofficially in international soccer and baseball.

I've never been a fan of instant replay. What you're doing is looking over the shoulder of someone you've given a job to do. The officials have to make the call. If you look over their shoulder, it doesn't help the game. As the referee says, 'It's nothing until I make the call.' This used to upset a lot of people. The officials have to accept responsibility. If someone is always looking over their shoulder, they aren't going to do it.–Chuck Noll

The reviewable plays fall in three main areas: sideline, goal line and end zone and end-line plays; passing plays; and other detectable infractions, such as a runner ruled down without defensive contact and the number of players on the field.

> *Officiating is not perfectible. There's always going to be criticism. I am consistent with my father (legendary coach Paul Brown) and do not favor instant replay. An infinitesimal number of plays were reversed. It delayed and interfered with the flow of the game.*–Michael Brown, president and general manager of the Cincinnati Bengals

The league officiating department reviewed every play from every game during the 1998 season and found only 77 out of a possible 37,060 plays that it deemed reversible. This is a fantastic percentage of 0.02 percent, but was done without the environment of a game or challenges by a coach. From 1986 through 1991, using television instant replay, according to league statistics, in 1,330 games a total of 2,967 plays were closely reviewed and there were 376 reversals, a percentage of 12.6 percent.

> *I've always been in favor of instant replay. We have the technology and should use it. I believe an official on the field should be responsible for making the decision. I'm not in favor of complicating it with a challenge system. Don't make the coach challenge the call. Let the official on the field decide.*–Don Shula, as coach of the Baltimore Colts from 1963-69 and Miami Dolphins from 1970-1995, he won more game (347) than any other coach in NFL history. Elected to the NFL Pro Football Hall of Fame he also won two Super Bowls and directed the Dolphins to a perfect 17-0 season

Reviews must be completed in no more than 90 seconds, timed from when the referee begins his review at the field-level monitor. During the 1999 season the average time of a review took only 55 seconds and delayed the game an average of 2 minutes and 54 seconds.

> *We are always looking for ways to improve the game. Our officiating is very strong, but our game is incredibly fast with a large field to cover. Our clubs are divided, as they always have been, on whether instant replay in any form is good for the game. This experiment is a means for the league to determine if there are satisfactory methods to correct the rare and significant obvious error and at the same time eliminate many of the disadvantages of the prior system.*–Paul Tagliabue, NFL Commissioner

The instant replay system for 1999 covered a variety of plays in three main areas. In plays involved sidelines, goal line, end zone, the following situations are covered: scoring plays, including a runner breaking the plane of the goal line; pass complete or incomplete or intercepted at a sideline, goal line, end zone and end line plays; a runner or receiver in or out of bounds; and recovery of a loose ball in or out of bounds.

On passing plays, the system gets involved when a pass is ruled complete, incomplete or intercepted in the field of playing; a forward pass is touched by an ineligible receiver or a defensive player; to determine if the ball is a forward pass or fumble; whether there is an illegal forward pass beyond the line of scrimmage or after a change of possession; and whether it was a forward or backward pass from behind the line of scrimmage.

Other detectable infractions include a runner ruled not down by defensive contact; forward progress with respect to a first down; touching of a kick; and the number of players on the field.

> *I am in favor of instant replay. In a critical game, a team trying to make the playoffs, a playoff game or a Super Bowl, there is no tomorrow. The players are so big and fast today and there are many situations where something happens so fast or an official gets screened out and can't see hat happens yet a decision has to be made. The official on the*

field makes the best calculated decision he can make. There
should be an opportunity to make a change.–Nick Skorich

During the 1999 season, 195 plays were reviewed and 57 overturned the officials' on-field ruling, or 29.2 percent, higher than in any previous season. Of the reviews, 133 were coaches' challenges and 37 of these resulted in reversing the decision, or 27.8 percent. The other 62 reviews were called by the replay assistant and 20 of these were reversed, or an even higher 32.2 percent.

Instant replay definitely has its role now and must be
something that is used sparingly and at the request of a
coach. There should be a reward if the coach is right and a
penalty if he is wrong in challenging the call. Every play
should not be subject to a review.–Harry Usher

But even all this with a system developed at a cost of $10 million didn't guarantee fixing all problems. Giants coach Jim Fassel was convinced that both human eyes and the television cameras failed during two critical calls in a pre-season loss his team had at Baltimore. One call was a fumble charged when it appeared the runner was already down and a 35-yard pass reception called good when the receiver apparently landed with his toe on the sideline. Jimmy Johnson and his Miami Dolphins were convinced that a 14-yard pass catch should have been overturned because a San Diego receiver was out of bounds. Johnson exercised his challenge only to be told there were technical difficulties that couldn't give the referee the view he needed.

Instant replay still sucks.–Jerry Bergman

Other sports are looking at instant replay. In mid-season 1999-2000, the NCAA allowed basketball officials to review last-second shots on a replay monitor after several controversial last-second game winning (or losing, depending on your team) shots. But when a baseball umpiring crew decided to take a look at television monitors to see where a line drive hit off the scoreboard and ruled it a double rather than a home run, the Florida Marlins protested. They played the game under protest and lost to the St. Louis Cardinals 5-2 and later lost the protest. It also delayed the game more than five minutes. And in game six of the 1999 Stanley Cup finals, the NFL used television replay to determine that Brett Hull's game winning goal in the third overtime over Buffalo was good.

Replay with McNally

In 1996, when Art McNally came to Morgantown to see Purdue play West Virginia we got together before the game. I even tried talk him into getting into business with me in my marketing company. I brought up the case of instant replay and told him what it could do to a young official who got a call reversed and how the official might be hesitant to make any more difficult calls. "Art, we might not get the guy back next season and could lose someone who had the potential of becoming an outstanding NFL official," I told him. Art said he never thought that instant replay could hurt a young official. While I didn't tell him, I thought to myself, "Art, if you had trusted your people officiating on the field and listened to them, things could have been a lot better than they were."

CHAPTER VI

Under Fire—My First Years

Sport has always been an important part of my life. In high school I played football, basketball and baseball at Weston High School. In college I concentrated on football and my classes in chemical engineering. In high school I was considered a major league baseball prospect but decided only to play my freshman year in college. I played first base and batted .407.

In my sophomore year, the West Virginia baseball coach had a scholarship player who was recruited as a first baseman. He asked me to move to right field. I told him I wasn't a right fielder, but a first baseman, and that's where I wanted to play. At the same time, the dean of the college of engineering said it was all right for me to play in one sport, but not two, because of the demands of the academic courses. That's when I played just football.

After starting the second game of my freshman year, and, with the exception of being hurt against Pitt in my next-to-last game of my senior year, I started every other WVU football game for the next four seasons. As the quarterback, I was responsible for running the option play. We were nationally ranked my sophomore, junior and senior years, played in the Sugar Bowl on New Year's Day 1954, lost only three regular season games and beat Penn State three years in a row. In those days there were no platoon substitutions so I was the safety on defense.

*Fred Wyant was a master at the option play. He would go
down the line faking, faking and faking and only pitch out
at the very last minute. He always got several extra yards on
every play because he was willing to take the hit from the
defense.*–Hot Rod Hundley

I had some great teammates who went on to the NFL–Sam Huff
(Giants and Redskins), Joe Marconi (Rams and Bears), Bruce Bosley
(49ers and Falcons), Chuck Howley (Cowboys), Stubby Krutko (Steelers)
and Gene LaMone (Eagles). Halfback Bobby Moss, probably the most
talented athlete of all of us, was drafted by Cleveland but when he and
Paul Brown could not get along, he became a career Naval officer. My
senior year, both Huff and Bosley were consensus All-American at the
same position–tackle. Huff, Marconi, Bosley and Moss all made the
College All-Star team that always played the defending NFL champions
in August in Chicago. We had eight members of the team named first
team All-Southern Conference. Sam Huff only made the second team.
Hey, what can I say? It was a tough conference!

In 1956, I was the #3 draft choice of the Washington Redskins.
When I signed my $7,000 contract I got a $500 bonus. The salaries are
certainly different today. Some quarterbacks make more than that just
for throwing an incomplete pass! And the $500 bonus now would be
considered "meal money." My coach was Joe Kuharich. I started three
pre-season games and then severely sprained my ankle. During the
regular season I was backup to Eddie LeBaron. Obviously I showed
them what I had during pre-season or I wouldn't have started another
game after the first. I would have liked to have known what could have
happened if I hadn't been injured.

Kuharick and I had a good relationship not only as my coach, but
when I was officiating. He was considered for the job of supervisor of
officials when Art McNally was selected. He could have done a
tremendous job.

In 1957, I left the Redskins to be the starting quarterback for the
Toronto Argonauts in the Canadian Football League. Before the '58
season began, I had a great business opportunity in Morgantown in

investments and insurance and decided that my future was in business as an entrepreneur and not a professional quarterback.

I wanted to extend my athletic career but at 23 was considered too old by baseball. They wanted me when I was 18 years old. My former college coach, Art Lewis, offered me an assistant coaching job, but after spring practice I realized that was not what I wanted. I thought coaching was too boring. I still wanted to be very much involved in football and began officiating high school games. I worked as many as seven games a week, beginning Wednesday evenings with my goal of someday begin in the NFL.

> *The harder you work, the harder it is for you to surrender to unhappiness.*–Fred Wyant

In 1959, I continued to work high school games and with the help of friends and former coaches, started officiating college games in the West Virginia Conference. This continued through the 1963 season when I also began working major college games in the Southern Conference, all as a referee.

I'll never forget my first Division I college game, before they divided into I-A and I-AA divisions. Furman was playing Presbyterian in Greenville, South Carolina. One of my duties as a referee was to publicly introduce the other officials. As I did, they would step out and tip their hat or raise their arm as an acknowledgment. When the time came, I looked at the other four officials and my mind went completely blank. I couldn't remember any names, but I had to make the introductions. I looked over and said, "This is Mr. Smith and Mr. Brown, Mr. White and Mr. Jones." To this day, if I ever run into any of these people they always look at me and say, "Mr. Smith, Mr. White, Mr. Brown and Mr. Jones and that we officiated a game together."

My big break came in 1965 when I refereed games of several major independents, including the Florida State-Virginia Tech game. This year I was scouted and recruited by the NFL. The AFL and NFL were rivals at this time and teams would hire "baby sitters" to help recruit and sign college players. Jack Fleming, who announced all of my college games at WVU, also was announcing the Pittsburgh Steelers games. He and my former teammates Huff, Bosley, Marconi and Howley helped connect me with the NFL.

The NFL hired me as a "baby sitter" and I was assigned to college players to become friends, entertain them and try to sign them after the draft and before the AFL could get them under contract. I let the league know that I wanted to be an official, not a baby sitter.

While I was working for the league, along with the late Bob Prince, the radio announcer for years for the Pittsburgh Steelers and Pittsburgh Pirates, I did help sign the Steelers' #1 draft choice, Dick Leftrich, who also happened to be the first African-American football player at West Virginia. Miami, then in the AFL, was also trying to sign him. He was being pursued by Rex Baumgartner, a friend from Clarksburg, and Marion Motley, the great Hall of Fame fullback who played for Cleveland and Pittsburgh.

Prince and I were in a cab with Leftrich in Pittsburgh and were on our way to get his signature on a contract when we passed another cab in which Baumgartner and Motley were riding. We hid Leftrich so they couldn't see him. I couldn't resist rolling down the window and sticking my head out and yelling "Hey, Rex! Hey Marion!" I don't think they saw us and we drove on to a tailor shop where we got the contract executed in the back room.

I believed being an NFL official would be a great asset to my career in sales. I could stay in athletics, have a prestigious job, and I knew I could do it. The fall of 1966, I began as a line judge and was assigned to Art McNally's crew. During that first year you learn how little you know about officiating. You are working with the best officials in the best football league in the world. It is tremendously exhilarating. You realized you had to learn so much more if you were going to be a great official.

> *Fred had a great football sense which is very important. He knew the game so well because he played it at such a high level, not just high school, not just college, but the NFL. He had so much experience on the field, he appeared relaxed*

and almost nonchalant during a game. He had an attitude
of 'I'm out here. I'm a quarterback. I've done this.' He gave
the feeling he belonged there and could react and respond
very well. McNally wanted someone that looked more alert
and intense.–Jim Tunney

I felt I had many of the qualities needed to be a great NFL official–
sound judgment, someone who could make difficult decisions, a hard
worker, intelligent, extremely high self esteem, athletic background,
very persistent, could stand pressure and I understood the game. During
World War II, my father was in the South Pacific for two years and
being the oldest in the family, I was given tremendous responsibility to
help my mom with my two younger brothers. My mom also was an
athlete and played basketball on the only state championship team in
Weston High School's history. My dad played football, basketball, baseball
and ran track.

I had been in business since I was eight years old and started
delivering newspapers and mowing grass. At 13, I was good enough to
play semi-pro baseball against traveling black baseball teams like the
Detroit Clowns that came to town. I was the third string center on our
high school football team when I was in the sixth grade and the next
year started on our ninth grade basketball team. In both high school
and college I called all of the offensive plays.

The pressure was severe in my first NFL game because I was
actually auditioning for a possible career and just wanted to get through
the year. I was being paid for doing something I liked and it was significant.
The NFL had a generous policy of helping people the first couple of
years by being lenient as you get on-the-job training the way they
wanted things done. Later, the pressure never concerned me or had
any affect on what I did or how I did it. It just happened to be there.
You either handle it or don't handle it. I was fortunate I had an ability to
handle pressure throughout my life before going into the NFL. There
were others, unfortunately, who couldn't handle pressure and eventually
resigned or were dismissed.

Any young official coming into the league needed to work with him. He knew how to make them relax. He was not an uptight referee and had enough humor and business sense to get the job done.–Frank Glover, NFL headlinesman for 17 years.

Art McNally was a high school teacher and coach from Philadelphia. He also was a basketball official. Quite a few officials came from that area, worked together and all seemed to have the same temperament. He had very little sense of humor, was extremely serious and didn't like anything happening that was outside of the game during the time we were together–pre-game meeting, dressing room and on the field. Our personalities were completely opposite. I did my job well enough as a rookie to be brought back a second year.

As I was starting my career as an NFL official, I was lucky to work with some of the very best in the business and learn from them. One person who taught me well in my early years was Bernie Ulman from Baltimore. As the headlinesman, during a game, he was directly opposite me. He had been a referee in the league and later again was assigned to be a referee. He was a super nice guy and kind to me during the seasons I worked with him. Rules and the ability to master the rule book were things that would come to you with time and age. Bernie was a big help to me on mechanics and my demeanor and conduct on the field. We worked together on signaling and had our own signals when we knew we would call offsides together.

During his rookie year, Fred was on very good behavior. He was in awe of everything. The NFL has a way of making that happen. It was later that he began to have a good time, enjoy himself, and became 'loosey goosey' until the game started. He was all business on the field.–Bruce Finlayson, NFL head linesman for 12 years

I didn't chose to select someone to be with every day or off hour, not because it wasn't a good idea, but it just wasn't my style. I had other things I wanted to do, although others given the same opportunity as me would probably have spent much of their waking hours thinking about how to better themselves and stay in the league as long as they wanted.

During that first year I know I was not considered a cooperative rookie because I didn't do all of the grunt work rookies did like carrying projectors to meeting rooms. I would have if I had been asked like a man. Art gave me a lesson about how I would treat other people if I became a referee. My simple philosophy in life is #1, be nice to yourself; #2, be nice to everyone else; #3, never allow a negative thought in my sub-conscious mind; and, #4, learn to convert (change) any negative thought given you by another person to a positive thought. If Art said: "Fred, you're doing a lousy job," I would first listen to him, be honest with my self evaluation and tell him how I felt, especially if I felt I was doing a good job. I believe we need to help rookies and share responsibilities. I worked to build a team.

All of us were given specific assignments so the work was divided among the members of the crew. My rookie year Bruce Finlayson, who was in his third year as head linesman, and I were given the duty of renting a car to get the crew from our hotel to the stadium and then to the airport. The first problem we had was a game in Cleveland. Rental cars were in short supply and, because some major convention in town, the only ones available to rent were two-door cars. This would have been fine the year before when there were only five officials on a crew, but this year they added a sixth official. Getting six big guys into that car was like the clown act in a circus.

The following week we were in San Francisco. The first thing Bruce and I did Saturday morning was to go to the nearest car rental agency and get a car. As we walked on the lot, there was a big black, stretch limousine. Bruce turned to me and said: "That's it!" I was only a rookie and thought he was kidding. We rented the limousine and figured that would stop the complaining. McNally and the other members of our crew thought we were joking until we told them to get in. They loved riding to Kezar Stadium in the limousine. We all had fun until it came time to settling the expenses. That was the last time Art assigned us to get a car.

Fred and I were the only businessmen on the crew. The other four were school teachers. When he realized I was serious about the limo, he said: 'Those school teachers will have a fit. It comes out of our expense account.' It was a real budget buster. We did it anyway and did have fun. Someone else took care of car rentals the next weekend.–Bruce Finlayson

Another assignment rookies were given was to find a Catholic church for mass before the game. Charley Musser, Al Sabato, Jack Steffen and I were kneeling in church and all of a sudden Al says, "Oh, my God, they've taken Jesus off the cross. We have to leave."

We thought we selected a Roman Catholic church but went to an Episcopal church. When Al said it wasn't a Catholic church we left and found another one in time for mass.–Jack Steffen.

Back Together Again

The very first game I worked was a pre-season game between the Los Angeles Rams and Washington. As a line judge I was one of the first officials to be in the middle of a play where there could be a fumble. Two of my closest friends were in a pileup with me. Joe Marconi ran the ball for the Rams, was hit, fumbled, and when I was trying to straighten things out in the pile of bodies, there was Sam Huff, linebacker for the Redskins. It was a world away from our days at West Virginia.

Fred was proud of his West Virginia heritage. All of us who went to WVU were. Each referee had a code name that the public relations directors of the home teams would use when they needed to talk with the referee. Fred's was "Mountaineer."–L. Budd Thalman, associate director of athletics at Penn State and former vice president of the Buffalo Bills.

Say Again, Fred?

During a pre-season game between the Eagles and the Redskins at RFK Stadium, Washington was punting on fourth down inside its own 20-yard-line. I then called my first penalty. I called many others throughout my years in the league, but none with the repercussions this call had. After the punter kicked the ball, I saw a Redskins player block a Philadelphia player in the back. The rules say this is clipping and I threw my flag.

> *Fred was right, but he was wrong. This is the type of play, if the clip happened, you just let go. You don't call it.*–Sam Huff

Stan Javie, a senior and very experienced field judge on our crew, came over and asked me what I had. We were working on the same side of the field. "You can't have a clip against the kicking team, Fred. Pick up your flag," he said. I told him I saw the play all the way and began to protest. He then said for me to leave the flag where it was. By this time Sam Huff, who was not only Washington's captain on the field but then an assistant coach, ran right up to Javie and yelled: "That's the worst call I've ever seen. Who in @#$ made that call. That's ridiculous. You can't call clipping on a punting team!" Javie points to me and says: "Ask your old buddy from West Virginia about that call." McNally marched off the 15 yards against Washington.

> *When I saw what happened I told Fred to pick up his flag. But before I knew it, Sam Huff was in my face and all over me. He changed his attitude when I said: 'Look, Sam, my flag is still in my pocket. The flag on the field is your old buddy's from West Virginia.' He stopped shouting at me, went over to Fred and was quiet. I had to go over to break it up and tell them: Guys, stop this smooching.*–Stan Javie

I never made that call again or allowed any other official to make that call.

Mere words are never commensurate with deeds or actions, thus fall short of adequately highlighting Fred Wyant's contributions to the NFL and professional football. All of us who spent time on a field with him were blessed by a uniquely committed professional who began his career as an NFL official and worked diligently until his performance elevated him to the ultimate position of referee. Fred's performance was punctuated by class and integrity and reflected preparation, knowledge, experience and responsiveness."–Bart Starr, Pro Football Hall of Fame quarterback who led the Green Bay Packers to five NFL titles including the first two Super Bowls where he was named the MVP.

I worked with Art McNally again during the 1967 season. The following year he left the playing field and became the director of officials. I then had the pleasure of working on Ben Dreith's crew. For three more years I worked as a line judge and realized my goal to be an NFL referee in 1971.

My first year as a referee when I walked through the tunnel into Cleveland Stadium I had a feeling unlike any I had had before. As a college and professional quarterback I had played in critical games, sold out stadiums and the Sugar Bowl, but here I was as the referee for the Green Bay Packers and Cleveland Browns in one of the most important games of the week in a jam-packed stadium. Just the thought of it. I said: "Holy Toledo, look where I am!" I was awestruck.

CHAPTER VII

Critics of the Game

There are many critics of the game. Armchair quarterbacks. Sunday afternoon coaches. People who never played, coached or officiated the game think they are the experts who know best. Being an ex-player, I could qualify to criticize a player if I wanted to. I could qualify also to be critical as a little league coach. But I could not qualify to be critical of a college or professional coach because I haven't had experience doing either.

If I wanted to, I could be critical of the officiating today, because I've been there. As a former player, I also understand what could happen on any given play. But that doesn't stop the critics we have on television today. The networks can give any former player or coach a microphone and immediately they become an instant expert on every aspect of the game. While they may know their part of the game, they do not know officiating. As far as I know, there are no ex-NFL referees doing television or radio games as analysts.

After I finished playing professional football and was beginning my business career and also gaining experience as an official, I had an opportunity to be the analyst for the Mountaineer Network that televised and broadcast all of the West Virginia University football games. In a short period of time, I was directed which way to look at the camera, when to look at the audience and when to look at the play-by-play announcer. Never once was I directed to be critical of the officiating or to be critical of either team or the coaching tactics, although I was free to comment about any of those things.

> *Everybody today is a second guesser. Officials do a good job. Television makes their job twice as tough.*–Johnny Unitas, NFL Hall of Fame quarterback for the Baltimore Colts.

Howard Cosell was one expert who knew everything about everything and everybody, but in all the years I watched Monday night football, I would guess that he was wrong 95 percent of the time on his analysis of what the call was by an official and the reason the official made the call. The ex-players with Cosell never challenged him and of course the viewers at home believed him.

The most prominent announcer today who doesn't understand officiating or the rules of the game is John Madden. He certainly is qualified to discuss players and coaching, but he didn't understand officiating when he was coaching, let alone now that he has become an "expert" analyst. He is about as qualified to critique officiating as he is to rank airlines by service. Madden coached the Oakland Raiders from 1969-1978 and became their winningest coach with a 112-39-7 record. He is one of the most popular of all television football announcers and unfortunately, the fans believe him when he is wrong.

> *We have some wonderful announcers but they never had a whistle in their mouth or a flag in their belt. They should be careful about criticizing officials until they know the rules. We get great coverage on television, but sometimes when the announcers have a chance to praise a really good call, they don't because they don't know the rules.*–Art Holst

Madden and I had our differences. Coaches are not allowed in the officials' dressing room. Madden had a habit of sticking his head in to say "hello" under the pretense of wanting to get the official time. But John always liked to have an edge, or think he did. As part of our pre-game responsibilities, 1 hour and 15 minutes before game time, my line judge or back judge would go to the home team locker room with the home team's public relations representative to tell the head coach of the pregame time and get the names and numbers of the captains for the game. My head linesman or side judge would do the same for the visiting team with its public relations representative. Madden barged in before one game and I looked at him and said: "John, you know you're not allowed in here. What do you want?" He fumbled with his watch in his hand like he was adjusting it or setting the time, and then look right at me and said: "I didn't know that. I just wanted to get the official time." I put an end to that by saying: "John, it's time for you to get the @#^%*$ out of here." Before he left, even though one of my crew members had been to his dressing room, I probably also gave him the official time.

At a game in Oakland, my umpire Joe Connell threw his flag when he saw one of the Raiders holding. Madden came on the field protesting the call. As I moved to get between him and Joe, I threw my flag. "What's that for?," he asked. I said: "Coach, you're not allowed on the field." His answer was: "I didn't know that." This was just another example of his not knowing the rules or thinking I didn't have guts enough to call a penalty on him.

> *Madden always had a habit of being on the field. You just couldn't keep him behind the sidelines. I was running hard down the sidelines following a play and ran smack into him. As big as he is, he knocked me flat as a pancake. I was really mad and got up and looked him right in the eyes and told him what I would do if he ever stepped on the playing field again. He was embarrassed.*–Don Wedge

A third Madden incident involved Hollywood star James Garner. I learned that he was always on the sidelines at most Oakland games. He was verbally abusive to me and the rest of my crew. I will listen to a player and a coach blow off steam and use profanity, but I didn't have to listen to it from an actor. During the game I went over to the sidelines and said to Madden: "Is he on your coaching staff?" John turned around and said: "No, he's the Hollywood star James Garner." I told him to either get him the #&$*% off the sidelines or to keep his mouth shut. Madden complied and I never heard another word from Garner. However, from Garner's experience on the Oakland bench he could easily have qualified to be in the broadcaster's booth.

> *I had to run Garner back from the 10 yard line to the Oakland bench. After the game he came by our dressing room to apologize.*–Ben Dreith

The problem with critics like Madden and Cosell is that the American public believes everything they say. This had no effect on me or other officials since we were not influenced by anything they said. It probably created problems for officials with the fans who believed the officials didn't know what they were doing. While fans would be abusive to the opposing players, and sometimes even their own players, they would really get on the coaches and officials. When these same fans heard officials being criticized on Monday television night and then heard John Madden and other announcers on weekends, they became more vocal and more aggressive. This created a need for improved security for the officials from the league office.

> *It was a rainy, miserable day in Atlanta and Oakland was getting beaten. Coming back on the field at halftime I passed John Madden and said, "How's it going, John?" He replied, "It's days like this you think you ought to be an official.*–Jack Steffen

Not all announcers are critics. One of the best and greatest announcers who came from the ex-player ranks is Merlin Olsen. He gave you great insight into the game, had great stories to tell about the era he played in, but at no time did I ever hear him be critical of another player, of a coach, and especially of any official. He had a great understanding of the total game and he knew what he didn't know, which made him even greater.

> *Say only nice things about people. If you do, you never have to whisper, ever.*–Fred Wyant

In the end, it was rumored that the reason Olsen no longer was broadcasting NFL games was because he would not go along with the networks who demanded spice in their announcing, and this spice included being critical of everybody but the league. In my opinion, if Cosell, Madden or any announcer decided to criticize the commissioner, you would have seen an exit quicker than that of Marv Albert's from the radio and television scene.

> *I'm a Monday morning quarterback even today. Instant replay proves that some calls should be reversed that never were. I would like to see them bring it back and do a better job than they did the last time. Mistakes will be made. Players make mistakes. It's all part of the game. Television and replay puts tremendous pressure on the officials. The league reviews the films every week and the office takes corrective action against those that make too many bad calls.*–Chuck Howley, all-pro linebacker for the Dallas Cowboys, former teammate of Wyant's at WVU and the only player from a losing team to be named MVP in the Super Bowl (Dallas lost to the Baltimore Colts 16-13).

There is no reason at all for an official to not know the rules. The league annually publishes for the media a *Digest of Rules* with updates on the latest rules changes and league policies so they can better understand the game. It also has a web site media can access for other information This comprehensive publication includes definitions for clipping, double foul, muff, encroachment and other commonly used terms; a summary of the penalties; details on everything from the dimensions of the field to how many balls are approved to be used in a game indoors as well as outdoors; details on timing; discussion on rules involving pass interference and what is and is not a forward pass; the duties and field positions of the officials; and a chronological history of playing rule changes. It is virtually everything you need to know about the game and something that every media professional should read and then review and review. With this publication there is no excuse for giving wrong information to the fans and the public.

The Coaches

The league office is very strict about any coach publicly criticizing the officiating. The reprimand from the league office can be serious and expensive. One of my goals in life is to have fun and be around people who want to have fun. During my years in the league it was not always pleasant talking to or being close to some of the coaches on the sidelines. As a referee my main position was in between the inbound markers close to the center of the field. For 19 of my 27 years in the NFL I didn't go to the sidelines to talk with coaches unless someone was thrown out of the game, I had to give them a two-minute warning, or tell them that it was their last time out for the half or the game.

During my last three years, at the line judge position, I heard all of the names I was being called during a game. I would say to myself: "I'm respected in business. I'm respected in my community. I'm respected in my state. Why in the world do I want to be subjected to three-and-a-half hours of people calling me everything you can imagine. Unfortunately, that's part of the game. I drew the line with a coach if he indicated that we might be doing something dishonest. At that point, I made sure the coach understood not to take that trend of thought one step further or ever insinuate dishonesty, because if he did, I would penalize his team, and if he continued, would have thrown him out of the game. I never had to throw a coach out of a game.

I preferred being in the middle of the field. In a game I had with Philadelphia, my line judge, Gene Carrabine, raced to me and said: "Coach Vermeil wants to see you right this second." This was Gene's first year in the league and it was early in the season. I looked at him and said: "You tell Coach Vermeil to go $*%&@#." Gene looked at me and then walked back to the sidelines. I had no idea what he told Dick Vermeil, but I had no intention of talking with him. Later it became league policy that you had to talk to the head coach if he had a question. But what is there to talk about? No coach is going to say: "Hi, Fred, how's the family?" He will berate you 99 percent of the time about a call. If it is a home game he will stir up the fans.

> *Fred made it very clear he had no intention of talking with Vermeil. Being on the sideline, I had to listen to him the entire game. Sometimes coaches will get on a rookie to see how far they can get. He understood the call but pretended he didn't so he could make a point with the referee. I told him: "Coach, he doesn't want to talk to you right now and the call was right." He then called both Fred and me a '&$*#&#^'. During a timeout I calmed him down.*—Gene Carrabine

Sam Wyche, now an announcer, was one of the biggest on-the-field critics of officiating when he was coach of the Cincinnati Bengals. Another was Bud Grant, coach of the Minnesota Vikings. Image sometimes will fool you. Not everyone is the quiet, nice guy they might appear to be on television. Grant was one of these.

Joe Gibbs of the Redskins had a reputation of being a super nice guy. Like many other ex-coaches, he became a television analyst. On the sidelines he had a superior attitude and his criticism was biting, cutting and sarcastic if the officiating and the game weren't going his way.

Here is an example of Bud Grant's behavior. The Vikings were playing the Bears in Chicago and his quarterback, Tommy Kramer, asked for a measurement on a play that went out of bounds. We had already moved the ball to the inbounds marker and he asked again. I told him the ball had been moved and Kramer again asked us to measure to see whether or not it was a first down.

With all of the commotion on the sidelines, I looked over Grant was yelling: "You made a mistake." I went to my side judge, Joe Haynes, who had his foot marked where the ball had gone out of bounds, right in front of Grant. He listened to the abuse directed at him and me, including Grant telling me how #&$*^& stupid I was. I asked Joe if he still had the ball marked where his foot was. When he said he did, I brought the ball from the inbounds spot on the field to the sidelines and said: "We're going to measure." During all of this time and the measuring, Grant's mouth never stopped.

> *Grant was always difficult. I went over to him one time and asked, Coach, who are your captains? He said, "You guess who the captains are. You guess at everything else." With his attitude, we decided to name the captains ourselves for that game.*–Don Wedge

If you've ever watched a referee on a close measurement, you'll see him look down to see if the ball has reached the first down marker of the chain. He then will turn to television, and show the distance needed for a first down either with his forefingers or his hands. As I was looking at the distance needed for a Minnesota first down, Grant was at my back the entire time. The call was close—only several inches from being a first down. When I gave the signal to television, I raised both my arms over my head and spread them far apart and stretched with my head back to indicate the ball was miles away from being a first down. Grant went berserk and yelled out that I was abusing him. If I abused him, I amused his team. The players around him turned their backs and broke out laughing. As I was setting the ball for the next play, Kramer came up to me and said: "I don't think you'll have to worry about us asking for another measurement."

The Pappa Bear

George Halas was one of the all-time great coaches and owners in the NFL. He was one the league's founding fathers, the only person associated with the NFL throughout all its first 50 years and coached the Chicago Bears 40 seasons for a 324-151-31 record and seven NFL titles. He began as a player-coach in 1920 with the Decatur Staleys who became the Bears in 1922. He again coached the Bears from 1933-1942 until he left to enter the U.S. Navy five games into the season, again from 1946-1955 and then from 1958-1967. There are few owners like him today.

> *Mr. Halas yelled and barked and said crazy things but you never worried about him turning you in for a call. He was a good, old tough guy.*–Jack Fette

Halas was a bear on the sidelines, not to be confused with his own Chicago Bears. Every other word was profanity. He also was a devout Catholic and used to go to church with one of our well known officials. They would meet Sunday morning and go to mass, socialize and exchange pleasantries between their families. During one game, Halas, objecting to a call, screamed out: "How can your pray with me in the morning and $#*$&# me in the afternoon?" I never had any incidents with him personally. I enjoyed him because he was so active at his age.

Another Owner-Coach

Another owner who coached his team for three years is Al Davis of the Oakland Raiders. He has been involved in controversy as an owner and does not always side with the majority on league votes. He was never a favorite of the league office but he had a good relationship with the officials. When he stopped coaching and became an owner he mellowed somewhat.

Davis had a great habit of coming on the field before the game when the teams were warming up. He was always friendly, called you by your first name, asked you how you were, how things were going, and lulled you into believing he cared about you as a person. What he wanted, was to get an edge. That afternoon in Oakland I gave him something to think about.

The previous year I had a playoff game in New York and Tommy

Hensley and I took our wives since it fell over New Year's. We did some shopping in Greenwich Village. As I was paying a clerk for a pair of shoes, he asked what we were doing in New York, where we were from, and other usual questions. When I told him we were NFL officials in town for a game, he said: "My brother is Al Davis. Do you know him?" I told him I would tell him we met.

> In my rookie year we had a game in Oakland. I was standing on the sidelines before the game and this guy in a white sweater comes up to me and says, 'Hey, Joe.' I had no idea who he was. He asked me how things were at home, knew where I went to school, talked about the coach and professional prospects of some players at Jackson State, and had researched me very well. Later he introduced himself as Al Davis. Other members of my crew told me he was trying to get friendly and milk me for calls.–Joe Haynes

So when Al came up to me this time, I caught him off guard by saying: "I met your brother in New York and even bought some shoes from him." He almost ducked like I had thrown him a curve and said: "Don't say that. You know we can't talk like that." He turned around and left and didn't want anyone else to know that we were talking.

Don Shula–Keeping it Man-to-Man

Don Shula is one of my favorite coaches. He would let you know how he felt about a call. He was as serious about criticizing your officiating abilities on the field as he was about winning. He would tell you and that was the end of it. He was not one to continue the disagreement by complaining to the league office. Don used to carry a little notebook of controversial calls he wanted to talk to me or other officials about.

> At the end of every game I evaluate my players, my coaches, myself, the game officials and then grade them. When I first began coaching, I used to talk with the officials and alert

*them to what we were going to do but it backfired and
ended up costing us.*–Don Shula

Shula knows the rules because he helped formulate the game the way it is today. For 20 years he was on the competition committee and worked hard to make the game as exciting and safe as it could be. Rules he and his committee helped put in place opened up the game and made it even more exciting.

In one television game I went to the sidelines to talk to the television coordinators and when he saw me, 35 yards away, he came racing down the field. When he was five yards away I started walking to the middle of the field. When he couldn't get his hands on me he gave me a face-to-face earful of what he thought about my officiating.

*I always found Fred very intense and as a referee, throughly
into his work.*–Don Shula

One of my first experiences with Shula was before I was a referee and was officiating as a line judge. There was no AFL, and the NFL was divided into Eastern and Western conferences. Green Bay, Los Angeles and Baltimore were all rivals and fighting for the championship. Don was then the head coach of the Colts. The Rams were at Baltimore and it was the 56th straight sellout for the Colts. A Los Angeles ball carrier was stopped by several defensive players, was shoved backwards, and then lost the ball and Baltimore recovered. The runner's forward progress had already been stopped and the ball blown dead at that point.

*You realize when you coach how many responsibilities you
have. You can't get carried away by things that just continue
to plague or bother you. You have to get your mind on the
game. I always reacted with officials, said what I had to say
and moved on to get back in the game.*–Don Shula
*Early in my career, Shula called me a $&*($)! I told him
that the next time he cursed me, I was going to call a penalty
on him, then turn on my microphone and tell the people in*

the stands, the press box and television: "15 yard penalty against Miami Coach Don Shula for calling an official a $&*($)" and use the exact language he did. I never had another problem with him.–Ben Dreith

I was on the Colts' sideline, directly in front of the bench, and signaled that it was Los Angeles' ball. Shula was right behind me and said: "You gutless #*$&$^)*@#!" At that time, I had only been in the league several years. I started laughing, turned around and said: "Coach, we're in Baltimore, in front of a sellout crowd, in front of your bench, and I just gave the ball back to the other team and you call me a 'gutless #%*^&@(#* '." Don turned his back on me and acknowledged that I was right but he still wasn't happy with the call. It shows how intense a coach can get during a game. It also explains why he is one of my favorites and why I consider him a true gentleman.

I was working a Buffalo-Miami game and in the second quarter there was a long play down the sidelines. I was watching the receiver and was at the goal line. The defending back dived for the receiver and completely missed him, but knocked me back so hard it tore the sole from my shoe. If I had been wearing cleats, I would have had a broken leg. I came to underneath the TV truck. The first person I saw was Don Shula leaning over me saying 'Don, are you all right? Are you all right?' I told him I thought I was going to be all right and that it was the first time in my life he had ever called me by my first name, even though he had called me a lot of things over the years. Shula had run from the 35-yard-line to the TV truck beyond the goal line to check on me. That's the kind of person he is. I was out for a few plays but came back to finish the game.–Don Wedge

It is hard for people to understand the tremendous pressure the officials are under or to know how hard they work. As a coach you understand being under the same kind of pressure.–Don Shula

The Good Guys

Bill Parcells who had successful coaching careers with the New York Giants, New England Patriots and later the New York Jets, is sometimes perceived by the media as someone hard to get along with, who is arbitrary, and rules with an iron hand. I always found Bill to be a very fair person dealing with officials. I never heard him abuse an official. I never heard him claim that we cost him a game. I think he didn't because his total concentration was on coaching the game and winning. Like so many other great coaches, Bill did not want to take anything away from his concentration when he knew that officiating was in the hands of the absolutely best group of professionals in any sport today.

> *Is Fred sure? I can give you names of people with the Giants and Patriots who would tell you that Parcells is a $*%(@#*&* and a %*@(%&.*–Name withheld by request.

Another good guy is Marv Levy, who coached in the NFL for 21 years, took Buffalo to four straight AFC championships, four Super Bowls and is the winningest coach in the team's history with a record of 117 wins and 68 losses. In both 1988 and 1995 he was named the league's "Coach of the Year." Until he retired at the end of the 1997 season, he was the dean of NFL head coaches, having served the longest tenure with the same franchise of any current head coach. Few professional football coaches are Phi Beta Kappas or have master's degrees in English History from Harvard. And January 2001 he was elected to the NFL's Pro Football Hall of Fame.

> *The only thing I would object to was over-officiating or where there was an over-interpretation of the rules.*–Marv Levy

More Class Coaches

Chuck Noll, who coached the Pittsburgh Steelers from 1969-1991 to four Super Bowl championships and a 209-156-1 record, never complained, yelled or was in any way abusive to an official. If he did want to talk about a play, which was an exception, he would request that he would like to see you because he had a question. When he made a request, I always went to the sidelines to explain the call to him. He never questioned calls that often and when he did, you knew he really had something serious on his mind. He was one of the true gentlemen in the league and his record speaks for what a great coach he was.

> *I can't remember any controversial thing about Fred. Any game that he had really went well.*–Chuck Noll

Another true gentleman was Tom Landry. I can't remember him ever saying anything to me because he was always so intent on coaching. I never heard him swear or scream at an official. If he had a question on a particular play he would ask for an answer just like Chuck Noll. Landry was the Cowboys first coach. From 1960-1988 he compiled a 270-178-6 record and directed them to the Super Bowl five times with two championships. However, he did have members of his coaching staff who let us know if they were unhappy with any of our calls. In a Thursday night game with Minnesota playing at Dallas, we called only five penalties in the game. This is almost unheard of. Ernie Stautner, one of Landry's top assistants, had been complaining to Tommy Hensley. Right after the game Ernie jumped all over Tommy who finally had it and said, "Ernie, just go #*%&^ yourself." Like a little kid, Ernie turns to me and pointing to Tommy says, "Did you hear what he said to me?" I replied, "But Ernie, you just called him a #*%&%^*!(*!"

> *I missed one season when I had a heart attack. The first game I had when I came back was at Denver and I was discussing my condition with Dan Reeves who had just*

had cardiac surgery at Stanford Hospital. We compared notes and suggested I might want the procedure he did. He said he would give me his doctor's card which he did after the national anthem. It was a really nice thing to do. The next thing I knew I called a Bronco for pass interference and, as I turned and looked at Reeves, he said, "Don, you *#($&^, I hope you die on the operating table." He was smiling and I knew he was joking. I contacted his doctor, sent him my files and he said the same type of procedure would not work for my condition.–Don Wedge

We had an amusing incident when Mike Ditka was an assistant coach for Tom Landry. A Cowboy was tackled on the sidelines right in front of the Dallas bench. The next thing I saw was the football flying back on the field and it hit one of my crew members in the back. When I learned that Ditka had thrown the ball, I penalized Dallas 15 yards. There wasn't a word out of Landry. At halftime, on the way to the locker room, Mike came over to apologize.

I thought it was a late hit on one of our players and was angry. I just lost it. As the ball came loose, I just threw it back at the field, but not intending to hit anyone. Coach [Landry] made sure I apologized for what I did.–Mike Ditka I don't remember the incident but I'm sure Mike didn't need any prodding from me to apologize. He did have a temper but has calmed down a lot in recent years.–Tom Landry

A great deal of criticism has been directed at George Allen who I found to be a nice person on the sidelines. Just like John Madden, he worked for every edge he could get. In one game, the ball was on the five yard line and coaches aren't allowed outside of a marked off area that restricts them between the 35 yard lines. I looked over at the sidelines and saw someone I thought was a member of his coaching staff standing on the two yard line and yelling out instructions to the Redskins team. I stopped the game and asked George if he was with Washington. George said:

"He's not a coach." I asked again, "George, is he with you?" When George replied "Yes", I told him to keep him inside the 35-yard line. Allen worked every angle he could using his great skills, experience and knowledge of the game. Allen, of course, was one of professional football's great innovators. He was responsible for the nickel defense, the dime defense, special teams and the special training camps.

> *Whether the competition is little league, college or pro, you can't have rabbit ears and be an official. You have to have thick skin. When you set yourself up as an arbiter, you're damned if you do and damned if you don't. You need to just keep your mind on the game and not worry about what anyone says.*–Frank Glover

Paul Brown was another coach who didn't spend a lot of time yelling at officials. He was another very intense coach, understood officiating, and would be critical about calls but never made it personal and he never dwelled on it very long. His concentration was on the game and on winning.

Vince Lombardi–The Perfectionist

Vince Lombardi was truly one of our greatest football coaches. He was a perfectionist, a very fair man, a great leader and shared my philosophy of living life to its fullest. After coaching Green Bay to five NFL titles and victories in Super Bowls I and II, he took a year off, but came back in 1969 to coach the Redskins for one season. For him, winning wasn't everything, it was the only thing. He would never chew you out unless he thought you were wrong.

When I worked as a line judge he would be behind me and question certain plays. "Fred, what happened on that play?" he would ask. I would tell him that the player lined up offsides or moved too quickly and he would ask: "Are you sure?" And I would tell him: "Yes." Then Lombardi would call on the field and raise cain with the player who had the foul called against him. He considered a penalty a mistake if it was truly a foul. If not, he blamed the official.

In his last season, he asked one of my closest friends and teammate from West Virginia University, Sam Huff, to not only be an assistant coach, but to come out of retirement and play one more season. The game was in Washington with the Redskins hosting the Philadelphia Eagles. I was still a line judge. With just about a minute left in the game, Washington had the ball on its own 40 yard line, first and 10. With a lead, all Washington wanted to do was run out the clock and end the season with an 8-4-2 record. The fullback fumbled the handoff and the Eagles recovered. Philadelphia quarterback Norm Snead threw three long passes that were incomplete. On fourth down he threw another long pass and one of the back judges called pass interference against a Washington defender on the one yard line. Philadelphia scored and won the game as time ran out.

> *The pass Norm Snead threw was so high that even Wilt Chamberlain couldn't have caught it. It was 10-15 feet over every receivers head–completely uncatchable. Mike Bass was there defending but there was very little contact. The penalty gave the Eagles the ball on the one yard line and they scored on the next play. When the game was over, Coach Lombardi was looking for the first striped shirt he could find and Fred was right there by the bench. He was all over him until I told him he had the wrong guy."–Sam Huff*

Lombardi exploded, ran at me and began screaming. Sam Huff was right behind Lombardi trying to catch up to him and yelling: "Not him, coach. Not him. He's OK." Then Lombardi turned away from me and started looking for the official who called pass interference.

A very angry Vince Lombardi stormed into our dressing room. He then chewed out the entire crew. As he was ready to finish, one of his assistant coaches took him out of the room. This is against league rules but I never reported it to the league office and neither did any member of my crew. Lombardi did not call the league office to complain. I treated him differently because it would not have made any difference. I believe there are times you have to make exceptions to league policy. This never happened again. Less than a year later, Lombardi lost his battle to cancer.

After the game, I was supposed to give Fred a ride back to the airport and give us a chance to visit. My wife said: "Why are we supposed to give Fred a ride to the airport? We just lost a game he was officiating. To #*$& with him. Let him catch a cab. Or walk!"–Sam Huff

The Players

Terry Bradshaw was one of the league's all-time great quarterbacks along with Joe Montana, Bart Starr and Johnny Unitas. Bradshaw, Starr and Unitas are all in the Hall of Fame. Montana will be someday. His complete concentration was on the game. If he had a question or wanted anything, he would ask. He never tried to big time you.

Bradshaw and I had one misunderstanding in the early 1970s in a pre-season game in Jacksonville. He went back to pass and his arm was going forward as he was hit. The ball was knocked loose and a defensive lineman caught it before it hit the ground. If the ball had hit the ground, it would have been dead but it was caught in the air by a defender. As I was giving the ball to Baltimore, Bradshaw complained: "My arm was going forward." I told him the pass was intercepted. He complained again: "I don't care, my arm was going forward." I again told him that the pass was intercepted. I was frustrated because he wasn't hearing what I was saying and did something I shouldn't have because I said this time: "Dummy, it was intercepted." He went crazy over my remark.

Later I learned that the Pittsburgh media had been on Bradshaw's case about being dumb and a country boy from the backwater swamps of Louisiana. He certainly wasn't a dumb quarterback. Just look at his record. He led the Steelers to four Super Bowl championships, was named the Most Valuable Player in Super Bowls XIII and XIV, passed for 27,989 yards and 212 touchdowns. He was inducted in the NFL's Hall of Fame in 1989. You have to be smart to accomplish this. Any other time I had a conversation with him I found him to be very intelligent, always in control of the game and never diverted by what happened on an officiating call, a dropped pass or a fumble.

Good listeners make the best friends.–Fred Wyant

There were four linebackers who were great and all are in the NFL Hall of Fame–Sam Huff, Dick Butkus, Jack Lambert and Ray Nitschke. The Bears could be behind 55-0 and Butkus would still be creaming people on the field. He never seemed to have the same kind of front line protection that the Giants and Redskins gave Huff, the Steelers gave Lambert or the Packers gave Nitschke. He had to take on the full fury of almost all of the blockers and eventually had leg problems because Chicago didn't have great defenders in front of him. I remember his sense of humor.

You have to enjoy what you're doing or just don't do it. I always wanted to have fun.

CHAPTER VIII

Violence and Sports–It's a Cruel World Out There

If my colleagues or I ever had a serious concern regarding our jobs as football officials, it would be over our personal safety. Our concern was not what could happen on the football field, but leaving the field or away from the stadium. Fans are completely out of control today and very little is being done to rein in and harness their outbursts. Verbal abuse is one thing. Physical abuse or mob violence is a completely different story.

Let's first look at what can happen on the field during a game. Injuries do happen on the playing field. There probably isn't a season that you don't see an official getting caught in the middle of a play and taken down. As cautious as the official is, how well he knows the mechanics of his position, how much as he anticipates how the play will unfold, and how hard he works to prevent anything like this from happening, he still gets involved in game action. Even if you had eyes in the back of your head, you sometimes still get trapped.

As a referee I backed off farther from the play not only to have a wider field of vision and to be able to see more of the action, but to prevent being caught in a blitz or sack of the quarterback. I got caught in game action several times, but will never forget the time I was taken down in New England and sprained my ankle. I only missed a couple of plays, but just long enough to let Joe Haynes become the first African-American to be a referee in the NFL.

Fans in the stands and the viewers at home watching on television get a kick out of seeing an official get caught in play action and knocked down. But being trapped in the middle of the game action in the NFL with the size of players today can be dangerous and even life threatening. And remember, we the only ones on the field not wearing any kind of protective padding.

The Umpire Must Have A Death Wish

Of the seven officials, the umpire is the most vulnerable. He is right in the middle of where the action takes place only five yards behind the defensive line. Every running play is coming right in his direction. The umpire is like the ball in a pin ball machine that gets bounced from side to side and up and down, and the players are like the flippers bouncing him around. As a play unfolds, the players are blocking, pushing and shoving each other trying to break the ball carrier loose or to get to the runner or the ball. The umpire has to be quick and alert to avoid being on the bottom of a pileup.

> *I got hit a lot but never seriously enough where I couldn't finish a game. My worst injury was tearing an Achilles tendon playing tennis at an officials' clinic. After surgery and being in a cast, I had to miss the first half of the season.*–John Keck

On a passing play, the umpire moves forward into the line and gets involved in the game action. And there are always situations where there is a draw play coming right at him or a broken play and the quarterback is running up the middle.

Tommy Hensley was hit a couple of times and suffered broken ribs. Ed Fiffick, another umpire on my team, also suffered broken ribs in a collision with players. Bill Quinby, who was my side judge the last year I was a referee, was seriously injured in a 1994 pre-season game at Green Bay with Miami. The regular umpire had a leg injury in the first quarter and by the end of the third quarter couldn't continue anymore. Bill came in from his side judge position and was fine until with two minutes left in the game. He was in the way of a linebacker trying to make a tackle and had five broken ribs, a punctured lung and damaged sternum.

> *Every time in my career I had to fill in for the umpire I got knocked to the ground.*–Bill Quinby
>
> *Both Bill Quinby and I worked with Fred his last year as a referee. The next season was my first as a referee. My umpire, Dennis Riggs, was hurt in the first quarter and had to leave with injured knees and ankles. I asked Bill to come in. He was hurt so badly he had to be carried off the field and spent several days in a Milwaukee hospital. Bob McElwee, who was on the sidelines as an observer first replaced Bill as side judge and then took over as umpire. I was beginning to worry that people would say "We don't want to be on Carrollo's crew."*–Bill Carrollo
>
> *Once when our umpire was injured so seriously that he had to be taken to the hospital, I officiated in that position. I had never been hit so hard or so many times in a game. Since, I have never been as sore as I was.*–Joe Haynes

No player will ever admit it, but some runners and blockers have used the umpire as an extra man on the field to get in the way of a defender or tackler. A very good broken field runner will even use the umpire as a screen to avoid a tackle. The tight end frequently cuts in front of the umpire and uses him to screen the defensive linebacker who ends up crashing into the umpire. The umpire has to avoid contact, but unfortunately can be in the wrong place at the wrong time, depending whether you are the offensive or defensive team.

> *In one game I was behind the play and a big Buffalo lineman hit me, knocked me unconscious and I hurt my hip. Jerry*

Bergman was working with me and was the first person I
saw when I woke up. I also remember hearing a coach cursing
me because he thought I must have interfered with the play.
After that McNally used to kid me that he was going to
reassign me to be an umpire.–Art Holst

There are a few, mean spirited players who actually want to hurt an
official or go out of their way to check, block or hit one. Again, the
umpire is the most likely target. A defender may feel that the umpire
was in his way and allowed a pass receiver to catch a ball or prevent the
defensive back from making an interception. This happened to Tom
Hensley one time and I saw exactly what happened. I was looking
downfield and saw a player hit him in his back. The flag was out of my
pocket immediately, I walked off 15 yards and threw the player out of
the game.

I have been hit accidentally and deliberately. In a Jets game at Shea
Stadium, I got caught in a play on the sidelines. I don't remember
anything that happened except turning a complete flip in the air and
landing on my back in a mudhole. I was lucky I wasn't hurt because
from what members of my crew told me, I really took a spill.

It's not whether you get knocked down, it's whether you
get up.–Vince Lombardi

Mike Ditka always had a bad habit of being on the field.
We told him to get back. His coaches kept reminding him.
As a line judge you can get crunched sometimes on the
sidelines. I was following a play and running full speed and
without any warning felt I had run into a brick wall. Ditka
was on the field and we collided head on. I'm almost as big
as he is and it was a jarring blow and down he went. He got
up and said it was his fault because he was on the field. I
don't remember him ever being on the field again the rest of
that game.–Joe Haynes

It's a problem being on the field with those officials
running down the sidelines. I've gotten nailed a couple of

times. Before I knew what hit me, Joe apologized to me. I told him, "I'm not supposed to be here." I'm just glad he didn't throw a flag.–Mike Ditka, former coach of the New Orleans Saints and Chicago Bears, first tight end selected to the Pro Football Hall of Fame

In a game in St. Louis it was a completely different situation. The defense intercepted a pass on one of the last plays of the game. As I followed the runner straight down the field, the next thing I knew I was two inches from the turf and run over by O. J. Anderson, one of the Cards running backs and a Super Bowl MVP. Had the game lasted longer, I probably would have thrown him out.

There's nothing like getting wiped out by Mike Ditka, especially the first time you are hit. The Eagles played at Pittsburgh. I was on the end line and waved a pass in the end zone incomplete. Mike was going after another player off the line and they both were still going at it, behind me, when we collided. I had ice on my knee all the way home. I was 31 then and had surgery the end of that 1968 season. I can't remember how many times I have had that knee scoped. I have had three total knee replacements."–Dick Dolack, NFL field judge for 25 years, now a scout and observer

I admire any official who wants to be an umpire. I also wonder about the people who officiate that position whether or not they really have a death wish. I'm also surprised that in view of the differences I had with Art McNally that he didn't try to reassign me to that position instead of line judge. I had both a knee and a foot that needed surgery. The last place I wanted to be was getting beaten up was as an umpire.

Early one season in Kansas City, I told Hensley that unless he wanted to see two officials get injured on the same play, then never ask me to be an umpire. He and others on the crew thought I was kidding, but I let them know I was dead serious when I said: "I'm not going to be an umpire. If you make me the umpire, I'll start limping, drop to the ground in great pain and you'll have to carry me off the field." Sure enough the umpire did get hurt in that game. Again, Bill Quinby was willing to come in to fill that position. The very first play he got run over and had badly skinned shins. In spite of the pain, he finished the game.

After the umpire, the two most vulnerable officials are the head linesman and the line judge because they can get caught in a running play. It is especially important for them that the sidelines be kept clear so officials have an opportunity to move up and down the field. There is a clear area on the field marked off in white but all too often players, coaches and photographers encroach on the area. We have to work to keep it clear.

> *When I was a line judge, I had a Thanksgiving Day game in*
> *Kansas City in the old ball park. It snowed the night before*
> *and the ground crew cleared the field five yards back. As I*
> *was backing away from a play, five Houston linemen hit me*
> *and drove me into a snowpile. There was a table under the*
> *snow. I broke my elbow.*–Jack Steffen
>
> *On the opening kickoff of Super Bowl XXII between*
> *Washington and Denver, I got caught when the running*
> *back was tackled on the sidelines. I was knocked into a*
> *woman photographer and her leg was broken. I was hurt*
> *but didn't realize until later that I had broken my tailbone.*
> *There was no way I was going to leave the game. I still have*
> *to sit on a soft cushion.*–Jack Fette

Players and Officials

Early in my career during a summer clinic, we talked about players not being allowed to shove or put their hands on an official. The discussion led to wanting to know how the league would respond if a player struck an official. We wanted to know whether or not we could retaliate. The consensus among the officials during the meeting was that if someone hit us, we could defend ourselves. Today, I believe that if an official retaliated against a player or coach who physically attacked him, the public outcry would be to suspend or penalize the official just as much as the instigator of the conflict.

People have asked me if I ever had a player or coach threaten me or physically try to harm me. It was my belief that I didn't have to worry about players because I felt the NFL would suspend a player for life. Times have changed. I would be very concerned today. Look at other sports and the violence that is taking place with players towards officials and even coaches. In 1996, Roberto Alomar of the Baltimore Orioles spit in the face of an umpire and later implied that the umpire was to blame. Rather than suspend Alomar immediately, which would have caused him to miss the playoffs, Major League Baseball gave him a five-day suspension that started at the beginning of the following season.

I applaud my fellow West Virginian Rod Thorn. When he was executive vice president of the National Basketball Association, he took action against both Dennis Rodman, then of the Chicago Bulls, and Nick Van Excel, then playing for the Los Angeles Lakers, when they shoved referees in games. The fines were the highest ever assessed players and in the $200,000 range. Based on players' salaries, however, this isn't a lot of money. Both continued to play the game. More than any other league, the NBA has moved quickly to discipline and levy fines on players when they get out of line.

The NFL has some strong policies today and spells out very clearly the discipline against a player for misconduct. The league says "Players, coaches and other club personnel must maintain proper respect for game officials at all time." This includes any physical contact like punching, shoving, grabbing or other intimidating contact that is deemed aggressive, or even verbal or other non-physical abuse such as profanity, other abusive language or gestures. This policy applied at all game-day locations, including on the playing field, in the bench area, the tunnels to and from the field and other stadium passageways.

The 1998 schedule for fines is a minimum that could include other forms of discipline with a higher fine, suspension and even banishment from the game, depending on the circumstances of the particular incident. For physical contact or verbal and any other non-physical offense against an official, the minimum fine is $10,000 for the first offense and $20,000 for the second offense.

The league office carefully outlines and defines what is not allowed, including fighting and even entering a fight area without any active involvement; use of excessive profanity or other unsportsmanlike conduct toward an opponent, game personnel or fans and taunting. The policy is very clear and in writing for anyone to see. And the league officials have done a good job in enforcing the rules and fining and suspending players who make moves on any of the officials.

Players now are fined for taunting and even a pose an individual strikes can result in a 15-yard penalty and a fine. A professional basketball referee felt intimidated by a player who stared at him and had him ejected.

Sometimes officials have to make moves on players. In 1999, umpire Jim Quirk actually tackled Jeff Robinson of the St. Louis Rams to keep him away from a Chicago Bears player. The Rams were penalized for unsportsmanlike conduct and Robinson was ejected from the game.

Because of his actions during the NFC divisional playoff game in January 2000, Randy Moss of the Minnesota Vikings was fined $40,000 for squirting water on field judge Jim Saracino. Moss directed his water bottle at Saracino after the official ruled a pass intended for a Viking receiver was incomplete. Moss was lobbying unsuccessfully for a pass interference ruling. The St. Louis Rams won the game 49-37. Moss had been fined $10,000 earlier in the season for excessive verbal abuse.

Kill the Coach?

Remember when Latrell Sprewell played for the Golden State Warriors and attacked and threatened to kill his coach, P. J. Carlesimo? The team suspended him for 10 days and terminated his four-year $32 million contract. NBA Commissioner David Stern then suspended him for a year. One of O.J.'s lawyers, Johnnie Cochran, rushed to Sprewell's defense complaining of "lack of due process" and "rush to judgment" and said the suspension would cost his friend $8 million. Tony Kornheiser, a sports columnist with *The Washington Post* wrote this: "Nobody's talking about choking the coach anymore, are they? Now they're talking about 'fundamental fairness' for the player." The dean of Fordham's law school who was the arbitrator reinstated the final two years of Sprewell's contract with the Warriors. What did the coach get? Sprewell was traded to the New York Knicks.

> *I never worried about violence from the players. The fans are the ones who are crazy. They are the ones you have to worry about. The players on the field are emotional and will explode, but they do have a line they will not cross.*–Jim Tunney

The player whom I thought might attack me during a game was with Dexter Manley when he was playing with the Redskins. He was one of the most rebellious and difficult players I ever dealt with. On a play when he came very close to roughing the quarterback, I warned him of a possible penalty and said: "Dexter, be careful." He lashed out at me and told me in no uncertain terms that the would do whatever he wanted to do and that I didn't have guts enough to do anything about it. I believed him to be very serious. He was mean, nasty, difficult all the time and had no respect for officials. He tried to be intimidating and my feeling was: "I don't like this guy." However, it had absolutely no affect on the way I called the game. If he fouled, I called the penalty. If he didn't, I didn't.

Later it came out that Manly was having drug problems and that when he left college he couldn't even read. Then you understand why someone would be frustrated. The next time I ran into him he had just returned from playing in Canada and was with the Tampa Bay Bucs. He was completely humble, a nice guy, cooperative and a person you could socialize with.

The closest I came to having a problem with a coach was with Don Shula, one of my favorite coaches. While we had our disagreements, Shula was the type of person who wanted resolve any difference on the spot and now, whether it was to his satisfaction or not. In a game where Miami played St. Louis, I had a rookie line judge who inadvertently blew his whistle. St. Louis lost the ball and the Dolphins recovered. The rookie went to Don Orr, my back judge, and told him what happened. Don came to me and said we had a problem. "The ball doesn't belong to Miami," he told me. "It has to go back to St. Louis. I said: "Fine. That's OK. Great job, Don, of coming to us to get it straight." I then went to the sideline on the other side of the field to tell Shula that the ball was going back to the Cards because of the inadvertent whistle.

Shula then accused me of lying. Knowing him the way I do now, I knew he didn't mean it personally, but I didn't know that at that time. I responded: "I don't care how critical you are of the way I referee, or what you call me, but don't ever question my integrity." Going off the field at halftime, the argument heated up again. Tom Hensley was in front of me and one of the Miami assistant coaches was between me and Shula as we both challenged to meet each other under the stadium to settle this problem.

> *One incident I remember very much with Fred Wyant was a Thanksgiving Day game in St. Louis. It was a very emotional game and I don't believe I ever got as tough or in such as heated an exchange with an official as I did with Fred that day. It was something that just happened on the spur of the moment. But what I remember most is that when it was over, it was over. We both respected each other, how hard we worked and put it behind us and got back into the game. I really respected him as a referee.*–Don Shula

When the second half began, no one said anything. One attribute I admired most about Don Shula was the fact that he could disagree with you in the absolute strongest terms but never called the league office to complain. He was a true gentleman in the sense of John Wayne. Another of his characteristics was if you told him something he didn't want to hear, he would just turn his back on you, walk away and make some remark like go @%#%$^ yourself.

I believe there is just too much fighting in sports today. Fights between players used to be common during training camp when offensive and defensive players got carried away with the competition and between one another. But what about during an afternoon practice before the final pre-season game? This happened when two Washington Redskins teammates standing on the sidelines went at it during a conversation. Wide receiver Michael Westbrook threw running back Stephen Davis to the ground and punched him in the head several times.

It really gets discouraging when you read reports like the alleged altercation between Michael Irvin and Everett McIver of the Dallas Cowboys in August 1998 at the team's training camp. According to newspaper and magazines stories that I read, Irvin, who was on a four-year probation after pleading no contest to felony cocaine possession in 1996, attacked McIver, 6-foot-5 and more than 300 pounds, causing a deep two-inch cut to his neck that required stitches to close. Irvin is 6-foot-2 and about 200 pounds. Texas District Judge Manny Alvarez personally looked into the matter and said he determined that it was a little roughhousing in the clubhouse, all an accident during a playful tussle over Irvin's attempt to cut in line for a haircut.

McIver denied that he was ever offered a financial settlement by team owner Jerry Jones not to pursue criminal charges or to publicly discuss the incident. If Irvin was found to have violated terms of his probation it could have meant up to 20 years in prison where he couldn't score touchdowns for Jones.

Behavior of the Fans

I've officiated games where snowballs, beer and liquor bottles and even money were thrown on the field. When people buy a ticket to any sporting event they do not have the right to be abusive. They are there to be entertained. To see the game. They can yell and cheer but must be civil about it. The ticket doesn't give them the right to be abusive or disobey the law. Sports officials in other parts of the world have been killed because of crowd reaction and mob or individual violence, attacking an official because they did not like a decision on a call. Fortunately that has never happened in the United States.

*I think that there is risk whenever you go on the field.
Football is a violent game. The NFL has taken measures to
protect us. We have had stuff thrown at us because people
don't use their heads and make a foolish mistake. I don't go
on the field worried about my personal security.*–Bill
Carrollo

Players, coaches and officials are concerned about being attacked by a
crazy fan on or off the field. A team owner has to be concerned not
only about the safety of those involved in the sport, but the fans as well
in the event of a riot or even terrorist attack. The 1976 movie *Black
Sunday* was based on a potential terrorist attack during a fictional Super
Bowl. No sport is untouchable and no event entirely safe from an attack.

Fiction almost became a reality at a Minnesota game in the old
outdoor stadium. Stadium security came to me during a timeout in the
first quarter and said they found some empty rifle cartridges and a
report that someone was prowling around on the roof of the baseball
portion of the stadium. I informed the home team and my umpire told
the visiting team. I walked over to Bud Grant and said: "Coach, security
has just informed me that there is concern of the possibility of a sniper
because empty rifle cartridges were found and someone thought they
saw someone on the roof." He looked at me, didn't smile, and replied:
"Well, if they shoot somebody, let's hope it's you." I said: "Thank you,
coach," turned around and went back to my position to resume the
game. In my experience with Grant, I found that he had no respect at
all for officials. Television perpetuated a completely different image of
him to the fans at home.

We have all been concerned over safety since the tragedy during
the 1972 Olympic Games in Munich. Coaches, players, officials and
their families from all over the world and in all sports have been subjected
to threats from fans. Most professional and college teams have uniformed
state or local police travel with them to games. Some coaches and
players have been escorted from the sidelines to the locker rooms.
Now, in some cities they are escorted from the airport to the hotel to
the stadium and back again.

No one will forget the April 1993 attack on Monica Seles. This has become the most prominent symbol of what has become the plague of sports in the 1990s. No one could anticipate what happened to Andres Escobar, a soccer player for the Columbian national team, who inadvertently deflected the ball into his own goal to give the U.S. a win. Fans were so outraged they shot and killed him in his hometown of Medellin.

The sports world was shocked when the Iraqi national soccer team, after being eliminated from 1998 World Cup competition, returned home and the players were beaten, tortured and thrown in prison. Odai Hussein, Saddam's oldest son and head of the Iraqi Football Federation, ordered team members caned on the soles of their feet, beaten on their backs and their hair and mustaches shaved off.

Soccer is one sport that has been plagued with violence and death. In 1964, 300 spectators were killed in a brawl in Lima, Peru following a disputed referee's call. In Glasgow, Scotland in 1971, 66 people were crushed to death at the exits. A 1985 riot in Belgium killed 39 people. Violence still erupts regularly in Italy, Spain, Germany, France, England and The Netherlands.

> The biggest fear any official, player or coach has is a riot with people coming out of the stands. I had a game in Yankee Stadium the season the fans used to sing 'Goodbye Allie', wanting to see the Giants head coach, Allie Sherman, fired. When I fired my pistol to end the game, at least 5,000 people ran on to the field. Even with extra police and security, there was no way to control them. We were all lucky to get out all right.–Art Holst
>
> When fans poured on to the field, Allie Sherman was running to get to the dugout. A policeman grabbed a man who had a 12" butcher knife concealed in his sleeve only a few yards behind Sherman.–Don Smith, sports marketing consultant and former public relations director of the New York Giants

During the first five years when I was in the league, the only time I was apprehensive about safety was in the Sugar Bowl in New Orleans before the Saints moved to the Superdome. The Saints were playing the St. Louis Cardinals and ahead with about two minutes to go. A long pass to Charlie Johnson resulted in a touchdown. The Cards kicked off, got the ball back, and defensive interference was called on another long pass. St. Louis scored to win the game. The home crowd was angry and began throwing not just empty beer cans and bottles, but full cans of beer. I have to ask, "Where were the police? Why wasn't anyone arrested?" But this is New Orleans.

Our dressing room was under the stadium. To get there, we had to walk through the crowd. In those days, we had no league security or police escort. You can imagine how we stood out with those zebra-striped shirts and white knickers. A fan walked right at me, shoved me so hard in the chest that it knocked off my cap, and then ran away. I was lucky I wasn't hurt. When we got safely to the dressing room, people began pounding on the door. There wasn't even stadium security at the door. Eventually, after we showered and dressed, the pounding had stopped and we left the stadium. Something terrible could have happened that day.

When the league began providing security, it was as outstanding an organization as I've ever been associated with. The NFL used former FBI agents who would call us on a Saturday night to ask about our plans, see if we needed anything, and make arrangements to meet us at the stadium. They met us in the parking lot, escorted us to the dressing room, and were around somewhere during the entire game. After the game they walked us back to our cars and saw we were safely on our way. If there ever was a problem, they would have handled it. Their primary job was to protect us.

In his rookie year, Tom Hensley was calling a Redskins game when a fan came out of the stands at RFK stadium and charged him. Tom saw him coming, turned and knocked him out with one blow. Police carried the fan off the field. But what if that fan had a knife, like the fan who attacked Monica Seles?

I was yelling at Tom to watch out. He couldn't hear me, but must have seen the fan just before he got there because he

> *turned and in one punch knocked the guy cold. Tom was a*
> *former Golven Gloves boxing champion and also a big*
> *guy. He dropped him like a tent pole. After that we called*
> *him "One Punch Tom".*–Art Holst

In my first year, Jerry Bergman was working a 49ers game when they played in the old Kezar Stadium. We had to enter and exit the field in a tunnel that led to our dressing room. Jerry had an entire bag of empty beer and whiskey bottles thrown down on him that hit him in the head, knocked him to the ground and required a number of stitches. After that, a screen was installed as security. I thank goodness that officials don't have to work in that stadium anymore.

Television provided a form of instant replay to league officials following an incident at a New York Giants' game when fans began throwing snowballs on the field. Television identified people and Giants' management took the fans to court and revoked their season tickets. This was one case where instant replay was very beneficial.

What team management must do is prevent violence from happening. Would I be interested now in going to an NFL game as a fan? Or taking any of my grandchildren? My answer is "No." The teams have created a monster of a problem by having tailgate parties and allowing fans to become intoxicated or near drunk before getting inside the stadium. Worse yet, when stadiums sell beer or liquor to fans, home teams are only asking for problems that will tarnish their image.

> *Football isn't a contact sport, it's a collision sport. Dancing*
> *is a contact sport. . . . This is a violent sport. That's why*
> *crowds love it.*–Vince Lombardi

Pro football is not totally responsible. The same problems happen Saturday afternoons at college games throughout the country. Alcohol and out-of-control, abusive fans, just do not mix. I have never met one single person in my life that I felt was a better person physically or mentally after one drink than they were before they took the drink. It is one thing to drink in your own home, in front of a television set, and not bother anyone except those in your home. But, that may even be a problem for some people. It is another thing to go to a football game and ruin it for those people who just came to watch a great American pastime and enjoy it with their family.

Philadelphia May Have the Answer

When Ed Rendell was mayor of Philadelphia he and Eagles owner Jeffrey Lurie may just have come up with the answer to controlling unruly fans. They reacted to hooliganism at Veterans Stadium during a Monday night football game in 1997 and made public their plans to create a "thug-free zone" during future NFL games. City and team officials were embarrassed with the ugliness and rowdiness that ABC television viewers across the country saw coming from the City of Brotherly Love. Rendell and Lurie decided to do something about it because families were complaining that Veterans Stadium was no longer a place they could take their children.

> *During a player's strike we had a game between the Bears and Eagles in Philadelphia The Teamsters threatened violence and to ring Vet Stadium with trucks and not let anyone in or out. It was a nationally-televised game. Arrangements were made with the city for a police escort for us and the team, but we had to leave the hotel at 5 a.m.! Our station wagon was between the team buses and we got safely to the stadium, without incident, at 5:15 a.m. We then had to lay around until one o'clock in the afternoon for the game to start.–Jerry Bergman*

In addition to adding extra security inside and outside the stadium and having undercover officers even wearing jackets and memorabilia of the opposing team, two temporary court rooms and two holding cells were built at the stadium. Municipal judges were put on site to deal with offenders. This was like a "night court" approach. The judges handed out fines and jail sentences. During the first game with this concept, 20 fans were arrested, the first even before halftime.

It also helped by stopping the sale of beer after the start of the third quarter so some fans could begin to sober up before driving home. This is a success story every college and professional team should adopt. Both the Philadelphia Flyers professional hockey team and the Philadelphia 76ers professional basketball team could take a chapter in security and fan behavior out of the Eagles' book. Safety is the responsibility of the team management and more owners need to do something about it in today's violent-driven society.

In his book, *Sports In America*, author James A. Michener has an entire chapter titled "Competition and Violence." Michener looks at competition and violence in sports from psychological, philosophical and sociological viewpoints. He calls football "the most violent of all games" and notes that certain studies prove that watching aggression does inspire aggression. In this chapter he continues: "In one American city after another, football games between local high schools have either had to be canceled because of threatened violence, or played on distant neutral fields, or played in secret before no spectators. Baltimore, Buffalo, Detroit, St. Louis have all experienced this phenomenon."

> *One thing I will always remember about Fred is that he always had a book with him that he was reading. He would even bring the book with him to dinner.*–Bill Quinby

We have to look at sport as a culture. To some people it is a religion. To others, being a fan or devoted follower of a team is the most important thing in their life. What really confuses me is how people can riot, destroy property, and hurt one another when their team wins a championship, a World Series, the Super Bowl or the Stanley Cup? Stores get burned, automobiles turned over and emergency rooms and jail cells filled. Today, cities whose teams are on the verge of winning the big one, at least are taking action to prevent or minimize the damage. Again, Michener believes American sports are especially violent because they are forced to reflect the inherent violence of our society. He writes:

" . . . because of our frontier heritage and our sentimental reliance on the gun, our society became somewhat more addicted to violence than others."

Architects and security experts throughout the world are working to design the safest possible stadiums. If they ever put a moat around the football field and brought us in through a tunnel, I would have definitely quit. I thought throughout my career that if violence were ever placed upon me that I would probably resign. I don't choose to do something for fun and have to worry about being hurt, harmed, maimed or killed by a fan in the stands.

CHAPTER IX

Drugs, Alcohol, Sexual Abuse and Sports Don't Mix

One of the biggest changes that has happened to the sport today is the anti-social behavior of the players and how it is tolerated by the coaches and owners. Not just in professional football and the NFL, but in all professional sports. Players get arrested for alcohol or drug abuse or sexual assault and continue to be considered heroes, at least by their owners and possibly even their coaches. As long as the offending players deliver on the field and help a team win, they will have a job. No one has asked the fans or even other members of the team their opinion.

There are few role models today that our youth can look up to and say: "I want to be like him." Unfortunately, too many young athletes are behaving like some professional superstars. You see this shameful behavior being copied not only at the college level, but at the high school level. The list of great athletes who have been charged with attacking their wives or girlfriends includes names not only from football, but baseball, basketball, boxing and even golf.

The problem gets worse when on-field violence spreads outside the game. Look at what happened after the millennium Super Bowl in January 2000. Ray Lewis, Baltimore Ravens all-pro middle linebacker, was fined $250,000 by Commissioner Paul Tagliabue for lying to the police and obstructing an Atlanta police investigation of a double homicide outside an Atlanta nightclub following the game. Lewis was MVP in Super Bowl 2001 and the first MVP not invited to do the Disney World television commercial. Rae Carruth, wide receiver for the Carolina Panthers was indicted for first-degree murder of his pregnant girl friend. A dozen other players were arrested on charges ranging from assault to sexual battery. Steven Foley, Cincinnati Bengal linebacker, was arrested for domestic violence. Wayne Chrebet, New York Jets wide receiver, and Keith Elias, Indianapolis Colt running back were arrested for disorderly conduct outside a Seaside Heights, N.J. bar. And a hotel party thrown by Dallas Cowboys receiver Joey Galloway to thank his hometown fans in Wheeling, West Virginia ended in a fight involving more than 100 people.

> *Character is something that is at the top of our list with every draft. Obviously, you never want to draft a guy who's going to be a problem for your football team and the organization and the community."*-Dave Wannstedt, Miami Dolphins coach

When I was growing up in Weston, West Virginia, and before I ever played even a high school football game, I used to read paperback novels at the newsstand that had stories about a hero doing something right, playing the game the way it was meant to be played and winning. Today, you can't find those magazines. Controversy is what sells.

One of the things I'm always happiest about is that when Sam Huff, Joe Marconi, Bruce Bosley, Chuck Howley and I played at West Virginia University, steroids or drugs to make us bigger or increase our athletic performance never entered into the picture. We didn't even have a weight room. If the university did, the coaches would have been hard pressed to get us to use it. Sport wasn't a science then the way it is today.

If you ever heard my seminar on happiness, you would understand why I believe life can be made into such a wonderful experience by just using what nature gave us and with mental preparation equal to the physical preparation that athletes put themselves through today. I've had friends who have told me that I should take a drug or smoke marijuana because it will make sex better and make life more exciting. My answer to them and anyone else would be: "How do you know how exciting my life is doing it the natural way when you've never been there?"

Before our officials group was a formal association like it is today, we went to the league and asked to be voluntarily tested for drugs. We said: "Look, there's so much to do about drugs today. People, football players and athletes in other sports are doing drugs. We don't want to have that stigma hanging over us. They could say: 'Hey, those guys are ex-athletes and may be officiating using that stuff."

My fellow officials and I wanted to set an example and good image for our rookie officials, future officials, and for our own children and families. We said: "Test us whenever you want to test us. Make the results public. We're willing to bet you'll never find an official who will ever test positive." We wanted the testing on a regular basis but the brass on Park Avenue turned us down because the Players Association objected. They were afraid it would embarrass and create problems for the players. We were denied a positive opportunity because it might put undue pressure on the players to be straight. What we wanted to do had nothing to do with the players. We were only concerned about the image we portrayed. We felt our proposal was a great way to present the integrity and strength of the NFL to the world.

The NFL has continually strengthened its drug policy, beginning in the 70s, through the 80s, and especially now in the 90s. The league and the union have worked together and today probably have the strongest and best drug policy of any professional sport. I would hope that is because football players not only are more intelligent, but more responsible than their counterparts in other sports.

There is no room in sports for drugs today. There is no question the league has gotten tough on drugs and should be. It is an important aspect of the game. You have to have good people. We were fortunate to have good people. You win championships with good people. You don't win

championships with pills. You have to have good, solid
individuals who want to perform and who are up to the
task.–Chuck Noll

Today the NFL has policies not only for drug and substance abuse, but
for alcohol, steroids, tobacco, gambling and even weapons. Everything
is included–performance enhancing drugs like steroids as well as the
so-called social drugs like marijuana, cocaine and heroin. The league
and player's union agreed on a three-step program for drugs that includes
evaluation and treatment before discipline and finally banishment from
the game for a minimum of one year. The league does provide the
medical help and counseling to help those players in trouble. But the
players also have to want it. A good example of how well it is working
is the annual Indianapolis Combine, where all of the top college prospects
are brought in for field tests of running, jumping and other physical
skills, as well as a physical examination and drug screening.

The NFL prohibits all anabolic steroids and related substances,
growth hormones and Beta-2-agonists, human chorionic gonadatropin,
diuretics and other masking agents and dietary supplements that contain
prohibited substances. All players are tested weekly during the pre-
season and with regular season and post-season tests and periodic off-
season tests for players randomly selected by a computer. Others are
tested if there is a reasonable cause for players with prior steroid
involvement or where medical or behavioral evidence warrants. Failure
or refusal to take a test or efforts to evade or distort test results will
result in disciplinary action. Players may appeal the test results and
even the discipline given them by the league.

The league has done a terrific job and turned life around for
a number of players. Every year we have a scouting combine
and bring together all of top college prospects eligible for be
draft. When we first began this program there could be as
many as 80 players out of 300-350 who had some trace of
drugs in their system. Today the norm is one or two.–Marv
Levy

Some players associations fight to be protected from any kind of regular testing. In professional basketball, they don't even count marijuana as a drug, even though it is against the law to possess or use it. This was at the heart of the players strike in the NBA in 1998.

> *How can anyone defend the use of marijuana? Or object to it as part of a league's drug policy? Using it is against the law. It's wrong. We can't tolerate it. Don't tell me you have to use marijuana to play basketball.*–Mike Ditka

Violating the league's steroid policy means a four-game suspension for the first positive test and it increases to six regular or post-season games for the second positive test. During pre-season it means a two-week pre-season suspension in addition to the prescribed number of regular or post-season games. A third test is a minimum one year suspension. And, the players don't get paid when they are suspended.

Baseball allows the use of androstenedione, considered by some to be a performance-enhancer, that is sold legally over-the-counter in drug, health food and vitamin stores and even by mail order. It is a naturally produced steroid that triggers muscle growth. Androstenedione is banned by the NFL, the National Collegiate Athletic Association, the International Olympic Committee and the ATP tennis tour, but allowed by Major League Baseball. Popularly known as just "Andro," the muscle-builder made headlines in 1998 because it was used by St. Louis slugger Mark McGwire when he hit a record 70 home runs.

Some physicians and sports medicine doctors have labeled it an "anabolic steroid." They say the steroid is a serious health threat and consider it dangerous because of side effects that can create personality disorders and liver and heart problems. Officials of the International Olympic Committee said they planned to lobby baseball and other professional sports in this country to conform with Olympic drug policy, including banning Andro.

The Dietary Supplement Health and Education Act was passed in 1994 and made hundreds of previously restricted substances available over the counter. These included powerful hormones such as androstenedione and amino acid creatine which are as easy to buy as candy. When members of Congress voted this piece of legislation law, they barred the Food and Drug Administration from regulating the so-called dietary supplements industry. Maybe we should review the roll call on that one, see who voted for the bill and hold those politicians accountable. Holding anyone accountable in Washington, D.C. would be a first!

The week before the 1998 season began, Steelers' offensive tackle Paul Wiggins was suspended for four games for taking the same androstenedione as McGwire. Coach Bill Cowher then warned all Pittsburgh players about taking any dietary supplements.

I challenge the other players associations, especially in basketball and Major League Baseball, to step forward and follow the leadership of the NFL which is premiere among all professional sports organizations. I would like to see the leagues work with the unions to further strengthen policies that would get rid of those who want to drink excessively, do drugs or sexually abuse women. Could it make a difference in the world today? Yes. I don't think they want to realize how significant it would be or the impact it would have on our American society. It would make an NFL football game be important to everybody, not just those associated with it.

There once was a time we had no drug problem in our American culture. As long as I can remember there has been a drug problem. You have to look at society in general. Better or worse, it is hard to pin point.–Michael Brown, president and general manager, the Cincinnati Bengals

I think it is great that the league and union agreed that no players, coaches or other employees can endorse or appear in advertisements for any tobacco products or alcoholic beverages, including beer. The NFL policy recognizes that the use of alcohol and tobacco is legal, but it states that "participation in ads for such substances by its employees may have a detrimental effect on the great number of young fans who follow our game." The policy goes on to say: "In particular, endorsements or other close identification of NFL players with alcohol or tobacco could convey the erroneous impression that the use of such products is conducive to the development of athletic prowess, has contributed to their success, or at least has not hindered them in their performance." I challenge every other professional sport to adopt this policy.

> *The NFL has done a terrific job in maintaining the confidentiality of players involved in a first offense and helping them with counseling. After that, the league has been very stringent in disciplining the players.*–Marv Levy

In his book, *Winning Every Day,* Lou Holtz tells how he started a drug-testing program in 1982 when he was the head football coach at Arkansas. He writes that he had a great football player who had developed several damaging personal habits and his primary problem was substance abuse. He adds that it wasn't as sophisticated as those in place today, but it was a start and enabled him and the university to guarantee to players' parents that their sons were entering a drug-free environment.

> *There is no question most coaches are concerned about behavior of the athletes. It's hard enough today to keep them in your camp without having to worry about drugs and stuff like that. Most coaches today are conscious of the potential problems and try to do a good job of screening the players in advance.*–Tom Landry

"When you are on a team, you have to trust that your teammates are capable of playing their best. No one can excel with drugs in their system. Drug testing (and the accompanying threat of suspension) provides athletes with an incentive to avoid this dangerous habit," says Holtz. "We can ignore the lures of drugs and alcohol if we are committed to excellence."

Behavior has become a problem in all sports. Professional football does not have a monopoly on bad behavior. John Rocker, Atlanta Braves pitcher, proved that with irresponsible and outspoken remarks that offended virtually every element of society. And Major League Baseball Commissioner Bud Selig fined him $20,000, suspended him for one-month and ordered him to undergo psychological tests.

Every incident involving drugs and alcohol gets magnified because an athlete is involved. This only parallels society. It happens. We have no tolerance for this kind of behavior on our team. We can't patrol everything. We can't babysit the players. But we can enforce the rules. The players understand money. We suspend them without pay for conduct detrimental to the club.–Mike Ditka

We see performance enhancing drugs used not just in professional sports, but in the Olympics and other Olympic-related international sports including track and field, swimming, weightlifting and bicycle racing. In 1998, the Tour de France jokingly became "Le Tour des Drugs" when a number of superstars and teams dropped out of the competition. However, what it did was put a cloud over all of the athletes in the race.

You find individuals doing reprehensible things–an entertainer, author or politician. They all become newsworthy items. I feel bad for players who are good citizens who get stigmatized because of a few. A great star athlete can be spoiled by all the attention and adulation he gets and begins to think he is more important than the average citizen. Most feel fortunate. Others don't have respect for their teammates.–Marv Levy

We heard for years charges that the sports medicine specialists and trainers developing the athletes in East Germany and the former Soviet Union were using high tech steroids and other drugs. Anabolic steroids, which are versions of the male hormone testosterone, are considered by scientists to be among the most dangerous of the performance-enhancing drugs. They also are probably the most widely used. This has especially become a problem with young girls between 14 and 18 years old. Their use of anabolic steroids has doubled over the past seven years. Some surveys have found girls as young as 10 years old taking the drugs. Taking these drugs for even a few months can cause damage to the heart and liver, cause injuries to ligaments and tendons, stop a teenager from growing taller and lead to problems in having children.

To try and preserve the image it once had, following the wishes of Baron de Coubertin who established the modern Olympic Games, the International Olympic Committee is planning to create a special agency to coordinate drug testing worldwide. Its leaders believe they need an aggressive anti-doping agency to address the drug scandals that have tarnished its reputation. The primary culprit has been performance enhancing drugs, especially steroids and various types of growth hormones that are difficult to detect.

Not only are players abusing their bodies with drugs and alcohol, but they are sexually abusing women. Some players today are completely out of control and the coaches and owners are not doing anything about it. I applaud Oprah Winfrey for using one of her national television shows to tell the American public how she felt. Unfortunately, in professional sports it doesn't necessarily stop with just the players. Team owners have been charged with bad behavior as well as sports announcers who tell us about the game.

Last year *USA Today* reported a four-month investigation showed arrests of college athletes are on the rise and colleges are increasingly facing tough decisions. The newspaper found that at least 175 athletes playing for the 112 NCAA Division I-A colleges and more than 70 football players on teams ranked in the top 25 had been arrested for a variety of crimes. The largest number of arrests were for assault, sexual assault or some other alleged act of violence. The reporters found that only 30 of the schools even had formal policies on how to deal with athletes accused of committing crimes.

Standards have to be established at the first levels of competition and athletes understand they have responsibilities to their teammates, coach, parents and themselves. At every level it gets more difficult.

College coaches have the last chance to straighten out the athletes before they turn professional. Some of the most successful coaches are those who have been the strictest regarding discipline–George Halas, Vince Lombardi, Paul Brown, Tom Landry, George Allen, Marv Levy and Mike Sherman. And in colleges, Lou Holtz, Bob Toledo and Bob Davie.

> *Too many athletes today have the attitude that as long as I can produce on the field, I can get away with what ever I do off the field. A lot of behavior happens because no one is in charge. A lot has to do with respect and how the coach handled it. You always knew Lombardi was in charge. Parents and coaches need to have tougher standards and demand the athlete meet those standards. Meeting the standards can't be based on athletic ability. People are going to do what the public will tolerate. Owners of professional teams and administrators at our colleges have to decide what is important.*–Lou Holtz, author, motivational speaker and coach at South Carolina and former head coach of Notre Dame, Arkansas, William & Mary and the New York Jets.

Holtz again tells a story when he was coaching Notre Dame in 1988 and the Irish were ranked #1 and scheduled to play #2 Southern California. He had problems all season with two of his best players who were notorious for being late and disrupting the team. "Lectures, counseling, threats, punishment drills–nothing worked," he says. He told them if they were late one more time for any team function regardless of whose fault it was, they would be suspended. The two were 40 minutes late for the pre-game meal against USC and he put them on a plane back to South Bend. Notre Dame won the game without them and Holtz commented: "I like to think that the victory was a reward for doing the right thing." All coaches with problem athletes should take this advice. It also is a way of preventing some athletes from ever becoming problems.

Role Models Are Needed

Do I want to be a role model for my children and grandchildren? Yes. Do I want to accept responsibility for that? Yes. Do I owe it to my children and others to be a non-drinker, non-drug user, non-steroid user? Yes.

> *When you get in the public limelight, you are a role model whether you want to be or not. You will either be a good one, or a bad one if you don't care what kind of role model you are.* –Lou Holtz

When I was growing up and then first started playing and officiating in the NFL, there were some great role models. Players people looked up and admired included Gayle Sayers, Sam Huff, Bart Starr, Johnny Unitas, R.C. Owens, John Mackey, Ollie Matson, Alan Ameche, Roosevelt Grier, Lenny Moore, and the list could go on and on. Young players looked to them as heros. These players never made headlines for doing drugs, being alcoholics, carrying guns, or being arrested for beating up women. Unfortunately, too many young children look to the wrong players as role models.

> *This could be a generation thing. In the past we may have had problems no one knew about. The league and the agents must do a better job of educating the players what it means to the game and their careers, and hold the players responsible for their actions. The Players Association must work in partnership with the league in testing players, coaches and owners. Just don't single out the players.*– Kellen Winslow

It makes you feel good to know that you had played in a sport and were part of a sport that developed such great athletes and also had time to be outstanding citizens and role models for all children. Where have these role models gone today?

*At Buffalo we were very strong on not bringing in a player who had a history of being a bad actor. We investigated, checked on any previous drug history and looked at each case individually. I didn't want to take a risk. When you do, you disrupt yourself many times."–*Marv Levy

It only takes a few really bad actors to give a team or a sport a bad reputation according to Don Yaeger, who writes for *Sports Illustrated,* and Jeff Benedict, author of *Pros and Cons–the Criminals Who Play in the NFL.* From a group of 1,650 players, the two journalists found 509 who had arrest records that could be verified. They found that 109 of the 509 players had been formally arrested or indicted with a serious crime and 32 had been arrested before joining the league, 61 after coming into the NFL and the other 16 both before and after turning professional. The combined arrest records of the sample group totaled 264 and included two murders, seven rapes, 45 domestic violence and 42 aggravated assault or assault and battery and other offenses.

*There are approximately 2,500 players going through the NFL every year. Fortunately, the overwhelming majority are good citizens, in part because we have taken a very aggressive approach to addressing issues of life skills and off-field conduct.–*Greg Aiello, NFL vice president, public relations.

Why have players given up being responsible and accountable to young children? Players are paid an exorbitant amount of money and do not seem to take the time to give back to the community. Their interest is in their own egos and the Super Bowl. Can the NFL owners and league office do something? I believe so. What would happen if the next time a repeat offender was discovered using drugs, arrested for driving under the influence, sexual abuse or otherwise breaking the law and acting in a manner detrimental to the image of the team? The team should just let the police and the courts handle the matter as they would any individual who broke the law.

> *If a coach has a problem with a player today, they don't get rid of the player, they get rid of the coach. Halas and Lombardi had control. No coach today has control. Coaches have lost their authority. It is very obvious in basketball.*–
> Charley Sumner, former NFL player and coach.

Owners should stop intervening to protect players like their property and give them third and fourth chances. Is a player actually worth that much to a team? Doesn't uncivil conduct off the field more than destroy any game-winning performances on the field? If someone has to go to jail, then let the athlete handle it himself and go to jail. As they say, "If you can't do the time, don't commit the crime."

Do you think Vince Lombardi, George Halas, Tom Landry or Paul Brown would have taken a player in the draft or traded for a player who had a history of abusing women, doing drugs or alcohol or taking steroids? I don't think they would allow such an individual to be part of their organization. Am I being naïve? I sure hope so. Maybe we need that kind of leadership brought back to this sport. It has been so great in the past, but its greatness now has been tarnished by the new concepts of liberalism, money, lack of civic pride and complete lack of concern with what brought the game to where it is today.

People have asked me what the penalty should be if someone is found to be a drug or alcohol abuser. I believe the playing field should be level. If you do not give the offender second and third chances, but no chance, the problem will diminish and possibly even disappear. Discipline in American life today as well as the game of professional football has slid backwards. Now everybody believes it is their God-given right to be given a second, third, fourth and fifth chance. People I have watched who have become great in whatever business they are doing are the people who were never given a second chance to do something that was wrong for themselves and the people around them.

The ownership in most sports today has abdicated responsibility for their part of the institution. They say that they have no responsibility for bad behavior or bad criminal violence on the part of their associates or players. It's a shame. It's too bad they are not acting responsible. I believe the pendulum will swing back. The general public will demand it.–Peter V. Ueberroth

Our society has become so liberal in allowing people to express themselves not only in words, but actions, that players have not been held responsible for what they do. We now have players' unions so strong the athletes are protected from being held accountable. After all, if they were held responsible for doing drugs or alcohol or abusing women, this might infringe on their rights under the constitution.

The last time I read the constitution it didn't say anything about people having the right to break the law, let alone flaunt it in the faces of young children. Who can say now if it's good enough for my star hero, then it's got to be good enough for me. There has to be a time when somebody strong enough steps up and says, "Enough is enough, let's get this thing in proper perspective. Let's start helping some people instead of falsely leading them in the wrong direction."

Teams need to do a better job of investigating the players they want on their team. The downside of this is free agency. Today a team doesn't necessarily have a long-term investment in the player the way Halas, Lombardi and Landry did, who could be more selective. Many look for a two-to-three-year window and the player being productive. If a person comes in with questionable character they can arrange to pay him less or get the maximum out of him during a short period of time. They say 'Hey, if we cut him, we end our financial responsibility and someone else will take the risk. We can use the money to pick up another player.' Others believe they can straighten out problem

*players and have them fit into the system. Others just never
get it.*–Kellen Winslow

Football today is a dangerous game, especially now that the game lacks
sportsmanship. Players try to harm their opponents by hitting them in
the face with headgear rather than just tackling or blocking. Instead of
just sacking the quarterback, they try to knock him out of the game
and hurt him. Players need to better control mentally and physically
what they do with their bodies. They can't if they are under the influence
of alcohol or drugs.

> *Unfortunately, kids are different today. So many are the way
> they are because everything starts at home.*–Charley Sumner

The league always flew us first class and I did not drink, but would take
the miniature bottles of liquor the flight attendant would give us. I
would bring them home to use for friends. My colleagues did also
because no official was allowed to have any alcohol–wine, beer or liquor–
once leaving home for the game. Ten years ago I stopped taking those
miniatures and threw out all of the bottles I had at home because I
wasn't interested in promoting drinking at my house. I offer my friends
a soft drink.

Only recently did the league institute a rule about taunting. It said
one player could not taunt another player. If one did, and continued to
taunt, it would be a 15 yard penalty or the offending player could be
asked to leave the game. The rule was brought about because of all of
the trash talk which some people think is cute. It is the most
unsportsmanlike thing a person can do, it creates anger and animosity
and eventually could cause a game to get completely out of control.
Celebrations in the end zone after a touchdown or on the field to some
people are just part of the entertainment. When you add taunting or
trash talk to it, it becomes a potential for causing chaos in the game.

In some regards I would like to see our policies more stringent. The counseling program is very important. The players association and the league have worked very closely together and have a strong anti-violence program. The colleges also are doing a better job of instructing their athletes on the evils of drugs.–Daniel Rooney

Our job as officials was to make sure the game ran smoothly, ran quickly, ran by the rules. When radio or television commentators say that an official "lost control of the game" they don't have a clue. The official can only take care of the things that are actually happening. If someone doesn't want to be controlled, there is very little you can do to deter their action. On the other hand, preventive medicine, not letting that kind of anger build up, keeping focus on the game and not what the players say or do to each other, will create the type of game I believe the NFL is looking for in order to hold on to their share of the public who pay money to see the games or buy the sponsor's products shown on television.

I ask myself how you can justify allowing people and children to watch a game as important as the NFL and not want it to be played naturally, without drugs. Today the officials, like everyone else associated with the NFL, are tested for drugs. When we first wanted to be tested, we even recommended that the reports be made public. The officials I worked with then and I those on the fields today are an enthusiastic group of men who accept the responsibility of leading sports to a higher level in the eyes of young children and sports fans everywhere.

CHAPTER X

Thank God for Coca-Cola

During my 27 years as an NFL official, a number of humorous incidents happened to me that I like to share with my friends and am reminded of by my colleagues. This chapter recaps a few of those.

One of my favorites is about the likeable "Mean Joe" Green, the all-pro tackle of the Pittsburgh Steelers. He played on four Super Bowl championship teams, was the NFL's Defensive Player of the Year in 1972 and 1974, played in 10 Pro Bowls and was elected to the Pro Football Hall of Fame.

Any football fan of the 1970s will remember the Coca-Cola television commercials that starred him. One was selected for honors by advertising critics as one of the very best commercials of the year. Green also had a reputation as a Coca-Cola spokesperson.

He always lined up very close to the ball and in one of our games kept lining up offsides. In this particular game, Green was called for being offsides five of six times, something that normally does not happen to him. When he was called for being offsides a second time in the game, he was so upset that every member of my crew saw his anger. The third time it happened, he went ballistic and I immediately stepped in to be the diplomat.

Me: Joe, what's the matter, guy? What's the problem?

Green: It's you guys. Whattya mean I'm offsides? I've never been
    called offsides that many times in a season!

Me: Hey, Joe, I didn't do it. My guys aren't responsible.

Green: Then who is? You're the officials!

Me: No, Joe, it's that guy standing on the sidelines with the chain
    crew. He's not our normal headlinesman. He's the one
    responsible. He's the one that's been calling you offsides.

Green: Well, Fred, who is he?

Me: I really don't know. He's just with us for this game. I think he's
    an advertising executive with Coca-Cola.

Green: [stunned expression] [silence] Well, I guess in that case he
    can't be all bad.

I didn't hear another word out of "Mean Joe" during the rest of the
game or after the game. Also, he didn't violate the line of scrimmage
again and didn't have to be whistled for being offsides.

Green was so irate that he told a reporter that he might do something
physical to the next official that called him offsides. The next week we
had Pittsburgh playing in Denver. On the very first play of the game, he
doesn't line up offsides, but breaks into the offensive backfield. As we
pass, he looks at me and says, "Can you believe that? I shot my mouth
off what I was going to do to an official if I was called offsides. That
should teach me to keep my mouth shut." He never said another word
after that.

*I was on his crew for five years and he always beat us to the
locker room at halftime so he could be the first one to get
the hot dogs."–Ed Marion*

Starting the Season Right

Unlike our regular season games when we had to get to the game city
a day before for meetings, for a pre-season game, especially one at
night, you could arrive the day of the game. I was on schedule and

ready to fly to Atlanta, but got to the Morgantown airport and we were fogged in. I checked the options about driving to Pittsburgh to fly to Atlanta from there and was told to wait in Morgantown that the weather people felt the fog would be lifting soon. An hour went by, then another hour, but I was confident I would still get to the game on time.

> *Art was really up tight, hyper and asking "What if he doesn't show? Who will we get? What are we going to do?" Fred came in his usual casual manner without a care in the world and looked at Art and said: "Don't get hyper. We'll get it all done." And he did.*—Dick Dolack, NFL field judge for 25 years, now an observer and scout

Art McNally was scheduled to be with us as our supervisor that day and I knew he wouldn't be happy about this at all. I also knew that with Art being there, I didn't have to worry about the pre-game meeting going off as it should and everyone being prepared. The kickoff wasn't scheduled until 7 p.m. and I figured I had plenty of time. As soon as I got to the hotel and checked in I went to the meeting which had been underway for an hour. Art did have everything under control. He was uptight and not very happy, but in the end, everything was fine.

The First Black Referee

Joe Haynes, a black educator from Mississippi, was my line judge for several seasons. He had been with me since his rookie year. The league was pressing hard to get a black official seasoned and experience to become a referee, the pinnacle of success in NFL officiating for some people. The league was "grooming" Johnny Grier to be the first black referee in the NFL. I felt we should have an equal chance in that determination. During one season, I kept telling Joe: "I'm going to make you the first black ref in this league. I am not Art McNally. I am not Pete Rozelle. But I will make it happen. And when I do, all I want is for you to let me lead the Alcorn A&M Marching Band at one of their games." Joe graduated from Alcorn. We all laughed and talked about it at almost every game.

Even when Joe wasn't on our crew, Fred did a great drum major routine in the locker room before the game. He always talked about leading the Alcorn A&M band. –Dick Hantack

Then the opportunity came. We were at Foxboro Stadium calling a New England game. In the third quarter I got trapped in play action. I put my foot down to mark a dead ball and a defensive player dived over the pile. My foot then was under a couple of tons of players and my leg flattened. It was the first time I had ever been caught like that or hurt in all of my years in the league. I got up limping with a badly sprained ankle. Jerry Bergman and Joe came over to help me and see how I was. I got up, took my hat off, handed it to Joe and said: "You're now the ref. I have to go to the bench and sit down."

The very next play, New England scores a touchdown. All is going well but I realize I had forgotten to give Joe my microphone and remote box for television. On the kickoff, Jerry Bergman calls a foul. Now Joe has to make the announcement and give the signal as the referee. I limp out on the field to give him the box and he is speechless. He has a terrible case of stage fright about making the announcement. I had hoped to stay out the rest of the game and let him really take charge and show the league what a great decision I made for them.

Headlines were made the next day about him being the first black to be a referee in the NFL. All of the Afro-American newspapers and Ebony magazine ran stories about Joe. Fred never heard a word about my actions from McNally or anyone at the league office, but I knew they were very unhappy with what he did. I would have liked to have stayed in the game as referee. With the help of the other guys I know in just a couple of more plays I would have settled down. It was a matter of collecting my thoughts and getting into the game. It all just happened too quickly. I sometimes wonder what would have happened if Jerry Bergman hadn't thrown the penalty flag when he did. I know Fred didn't want me to be uncomfortable and that's why he limped back on to the field.–Joe Haynes

When I was his line judge, I was the only minority on Fred's crew. I was the brunt of a lot of jokes but Fred and I were personal friends and he could says things and implicate me that people would laugh at, but if anyone else said the same thing I would have taken offense. He even ordered watermelon for me at one restaurant and the waitress was shocked. Another time, one of our veteran observers from the league office came into our dressing room in New York before a game between the Giants and Cowboys. We all got two passes for every game. The observer came into the dressing room complaining about his tickets. He didn't realize I was one of the officials when he asked if anyone had a better ticket because his wife was sitting up in 'nigger heaven.' Fred would not let him leave the dressing room without apologizing to me.–Wilson Gosier

During the week, Joe Haynes called me and said Johnny Grier called him and wanted to know what happened. When he called me to talk about it, I told Joe: "You tell Johnny Grier to @$%#^&* himself. And also tell him that if he is named a referee, he will always have to have an asterisk beside his name, because you were the first." I then added: "Remember, Joe, I am your modern Abraham Lincoln and I am ready to lead the Alcorn A&M Marching Band."

My Last Media Interview

During a Green Bay game in Milwaukee, the league asked us to meet with a reporter who wanted to do a story about officials. One of the main questions the reporter had was: "There must be tremendous pressure on you officiating an NFL game." My response was: "No, not really. There is much more pressure on our jobs at home than the

NFL. We look forward to every weekend and officiating a game because this is something we like to do."

I then supported what I said by pointing out that Donnie Orr, my field judge, owns and operates a multimillion dollar business in Nashville. I told him that Jack Steffen, my back judge, was director of engineering at Eastern Airlines and responsible for maintenance worldwide. After 15 years with Eastern, he was an executive with Boeing for more than 10. I noted that Leo Miles, my head linesman was the athletic director at Howard University and responsible for a major budget and programs for coaches and student athletes. And I told him how I was running 19 property and casualty insurance agencies and was a regional sales director for Franklin Life Insurance Company. I had nearly 100 people working for me and during the last 16 years, 27 of them were "national leaders" meaning each was either #1 or #2 in their division.

"We look forward to getting together, being together, and working the games before getting back to our regular jobs; but this does not mean we are not serious on the field," I told the reporter. This was not what the league wanted me to say. They felt I should have said that officiating an NFL game is the most important thing in our lives. I was never asked by the league to ever do another media interview.

Me, Ditka and Aliquippa

Mike Ditka is a super guy and a very fair and great coach. He was from Aliquippa, Pennsylvania. I happened to be speaking at his old high school and they gave m a black cap with *Quips* in red letters. Two weeks later my assignment was a game in Chicago. Jerry Bergman had known Ditka for years. He used to be a baseball umpire when Ditka played semi-pro baseball. They had a good rapport. As the teams warmed up pre-game, Bergman walked out to talk with Ditka. He points over to me and I turned around wearing the Aliquippa High School cap that I sneaked on to the field. Bergman says: "Coach, what do you think of that guy over there?" Ditka broke out laughing and said: "One thing for sure, the Quips are better players than the #%!& that I have here!"

I felt that was just part of the game. The league would not have thought it was funny and had they known, or the opposing coach complained, Jerry and I could have been fined or suspended. The league would have had 90 reasons why we shouldn't have done what we did.

My first reaction when I saw my high school cap was 'Why does he have that on?' Then I realized Fred was just pulling my leg. He's really a good guy and we used to have a lot of fun. People today get so uptight about such things.–Mike Ditka

Racing Payton

Jerry Bergman liked to have as much fun as I did. I guess that's why we worked so well as a team. He and I loved to kid the Bears' great running back, Walter Payton, and Olympian Willie Gault, a wide receiver. Every time we had one of their games, we would go up to the two of them during the pre-game warmup and suggest having a race–Jerry and me against Payton and Gault. We laughed about racing 100 yards down the field. To further goad them, I said: "You both better get pairs of goggles to wear because of the dust you'll be eating from Jerry and me." Everybody around laughed. Again, the league would have frowned on this.

Bergman had no chance. Payton could have beaten him running backwards!–Mike Ditka

Who Me? Holding?

Conrad Dobler of the St. Louis Cardinals was one of the first great offensive linemen. The adjectives I would use to describe him were generally reserved for defensive linemen. I don't mean that he was just a better blocker, because he could pull better and protect the quarterback better than other offensive linemen before him. He also was mean like defensive players. Early in one game I said to him: "Conrad, let go of that guy." He was absolutely puzzled and asked: "How did you know I was holding that guy? How did you know?" I told him that I look at the center and guard on every play and it is one of my mechanics. He wasn't called for holding the entire game.

While he had a reputation for being a cheap shot artist, I didn't find that to be true at all. But it almost created a riot on Thanksgiving Day when Miami played at St. Louis. After one play, as the ball was being blown dead, the entire Miami defense ran up and hit Dobler. Then his teammates came to his rescue and we almost had a riot. From the sidelines, Don Shula yelled to me: "Fred, get in there and break that up!" I looked at him and replied: "Coach, there's no anchor on your hind end. You get in and break it up. I'm taking numbers."

And More Holding

In my early years as line judge, I had a game in Baltimore when Weeb Ewbank was coach of the Colts. During one game he kept screaming at me, "Call holding on number 75. . . . 75 is holding!" He did that for the entire first half.

At the break as we all were heading to our dressing rooms, his assistant coach, Dick Stanfel, an all-pro guard, a good friend and former teammate, says, "Hey, Fred, we think number 75 is holding and Weeb's really irate."

We came back and were five minutes into the second half when I threw the flag and called holding. I called number 75 and looked over at Weeb and tell him "I got him Weeb. I got number 75." He screamed back at me, "Not our number 75, their 75."

Another holding incident involved Deacon Jones, a great defensive end for the Los Angeles Rams, and Forrest Gregg, a great tackle for Green Bay. The game was in the Los Angeles Coliseum and Deacon yells at me "Forrest is holding me." I turn to Forrest and say, "Forrest, are you holding Deacon?" Deacon says to me, "Don't ask him, he's not going to tell the truth."

During one of the many games I refereed involving Pittsburgh, the Steelers great defensive end, L.C. Greenwood came to me and said,

"Fred, these people are holding me." I took one look at him and said, "L.C. there is no one big enough in this league to hold you."

A Lesson In Diversity

Frank Glover, a head linesman for 17 years and a super nice guy, became a good friend. He was never a member of my crew but we worked some pre-season games together. We had a night game in Jacksonville. Both of us were really hungry and wanted to get something to eat before we went to bed. Frank said a friend of his owned a great barbecue restaurant that was located in a shopping center. As we drove into this enormous parking lot, there were hundreds of people everywhere, all of them black. There were few businesses in this mall. Most were clubs and the dancing seemed to be ending.

As Frank and I walked through this sea of people, I couldn't help feel them looking at me and thinking: "What is he doing here?" When we walked in the restaurant it also was filled with people. I was not only the only white person in the restaurant, I was the only white person in the entire shopping mall! And late on a Saturday night. The only table was right by the front window and people outside were looking in and also pounding on the glass.

I was very uncomfortable and couldn't appreciate how good the barbecue really was. When we finished, Frank and I went into the kitchen to thank his friend. Everybody was staring at me as we walked through the restaurant. When we got to the front door, Frank says: "After you." My first thought was that he was going to let me out into the crowd and then close the door! As we walked through the crowd, the people just parted. No one said anything. I thought there might be trouble when we got to the car because a person was sitting on it. He just jumped off, we got in and drove off.

This gave me the first experience of knowing what a black person goes through when they go into an all-white area. It was a completely different feeling. I said to Frank: "Was that any problem for you, Frank?" When he said "No", I responded, "The *%&$#* it wasn't. I felt like an albatross around your neck." I believe I understood how Frank might have felt if the situation was reversed and we had gone to an all-white place late on a Saturday night in Alabama or Mississippi. In the end, I don't know who was the happiest to get out of there–Frank or me.

*I know he was concerned how people would react. He is that kind of a person. When we got back to the hotel, I said: 'Freddie, I don't know how you felt, but I felt badly for you.' He is one of the nicest and most genuine people I ever knew.–*Frank Glover

Fore!

When I was on Ben Dreith's crew, we had a game in Miami and were staying in a resort hotel that had individual cabins and a golf course. Ben and Stan Javie decided to play golf and asked me to join them. I wasn't that interested in playing golf, but decided to play with them. Here is how Stan Javie tells the story:

Javie: Fred was a natural athlete and natural in anything athletic. But he never took it seriously. When we had an officials' golf tournament, Fred was usually one of the best players. We asked him to join us and he said something about playing tennis. As we were playing our round, Ben and I were ready to tee-off on a hole that was tree-lined all the way down the right side of the fairway. I got off a good drive and the ball landed on the right side of the fairway near the trees. As Ben was ready to tee off, I was putting my club away, and he yells out: "Did you see that? Some guy just ran out from the trees, grabbed your ball, Stan, and ran away!" I told Ben I thought he must be seeing things and if he did see a guy, he certainly wouldn't pick up my golf ball. Ben got off a great drive that went beyond mine, right in the fairway on the right side. The same thing happened. We saw this guy run out of the woods, grab the ball, and run away. This was too much for Ben. He immediately took off

*running down the fairway and into the woods. He was
always in tremendous condition and fast. I was worried
what he might encounter and I jogged after him so there
would at least be two of us in case the guy was really crazy.
"We went walking through the woods looking for the culprit
and all of a sudden standing behind one large tree with our
golf balls was Fred Wyant! I look at Ben and say: "How
about that *$&%*@)!"*

A Missed Opportunity

I had a playoff game in San Francisco, but was only the alternate to fill
in for any official, regardless of position, who might get injured. In the
last quarter, Leo Miles either pulled a muscle or twisted his leg. Timeout
was called while they looked at Leo. Then alternates were paid only
half of what officials on the field were paid. However, if I went in only
for one play, I would have doubled my paycheck. I not only wanted the
money, but to have been on the field for a playoff game. I even had my
jacket off, ready to go on the field, when Leo decided to stay in the
game.

*I told Leo 'Let Fred go in even if it is just for one play so he
will get full game pay.' Fred was ready, was unzipping his
jacket and was counting the money. Leo insisted on
finishing the game and Fred didn't get in at all.–Stan Javie*

Talk About Wrong Way Corrigan

There is nothing like making a fool of yourself on national television.
We had a very important game in San Francisco with the 49ers in first
place and Atlanta in second. A 49ers win would eliminate Atlanta from
winning the division. We had just come off one of the best games we
had ever called the previous Thursday on network television in Dallas
with Minnesota. We called only five penalties the entire game.

We're into the second quarter of the 49ers-Falcons game and had no penalties in the first quarter. Wilson Gosier threw a flag and I go over to him and he tells me it is for holding. I grab the ball and run 15 yards down the field and turn to the television cameras to give the signal. I look back down the field where the line of scrimmage should be and it's 30 yards away. I ran the wrong way!

As I was going the wrong way, Bob Wortman, one of my deep officials, asked other members of the crew, "Where in #*%&^ is he going?" Another said, "Don't worry, he'll be back." So, there I was on national television walking 30 yards just to get back to the line of scrimmage where the penalty would be correctly marked off.

This game has a funny way of humbling you sometimes, just when you think you've got everything under control.

A Polish Joke!

We were in Philadelphia when Ron Jaworski was the quarterback for the Eagles. He was very upset on one call and started venting his anger in a foreign language. Stan Javie walked in toward Jaworski and said a few words in the same language. I knew Javie was of Polish background and I assumed Jaworski was and they must have been speaking in Polish. Jaworski was cursing in Polish and Javie told him back in Polish if he did it again it would cost him 15 yards. Was Jaworski ever surprised. He was quiet the rest of the game.

All-American But Not All-Conference

During my junior and senior years at West Virginia University, Rene A. Henry, the author of this book, was our sports information director. It was his first job right out of college. He was the one who told the media about our achievements and convinced the sports writers and broadcasters to cast their ballots for us on various all-Conference and all-America teams and also keep the team nationally ranked in the top 20 or higher.

The 1955 season was our senior year. Rene was working to get both Sam Huff and Bruce Bosley named first team All-American at the same position, tackle, as well as recognition for me, Joe Marconi, our halfback, and a young sophomore guard named Chuck Howley. Huff is in the NFL Hall of Fame and one of the league's greatest linebackers. Bosley went on to play center for the San Francisco 49ers, Marconi was a great running back for the Los Angeles Rams and Howley became one of the Dallas Cowboys' all-time great linemen.

When they counted all of the ballots, Huff and Bosley both were consensus all-American. Sam had been named first team on seven different All-American teams. But when the All-Southern Conference team was named, Sam was only on the second team! And we had eight WVU players on the first team, but not Sam.

It has been nearly 50 years now and Sam has never let Rene forget that. But he always loves to tell the joke when he is making a speech. "I never had the PR support I needed when I was in college. I had to do all the work myself. With my hard work, I made seven first team all-America teams," he says. "The only job my sports information director, Rene Henry, had to do, was get me on the all-Southern Conference team. And you know what? He couldn't even do that! What kind of a PR man is that?"

We used to kid Rene about William & Mary, where he went to college. But what Sam never knew was that the player who beat Sam out for first team all-Southern Conference was Jerry Sazio of William & Mary. Not only was he a friend of Rene's, I later found out that Sazio was his fraternity brother! What is really ironic, is that Rene kept nominating Jerry Sazio every year to be in William & Mary's Sports Hall of Fame.

Sam loves telling that story. He says since he's gotten away with it for more than so many years now, that I should blame Rene for my not being named to referee the Super Bowl. Why not? Finally frustrated with the William & Mary selection committee, Rene asked Sam and me to write letters of support for Jerry. It worked and he was inducted into his alma mater's Sports Hall of Fame in 2000.

Bobby Knight, That's A Big 'T' On You

Bob Wortman, who was a field judge on my crew for a number of years, also was the supervisor of Big 10 basketball officials. I always kidded him about the antics and behavior of Indiana's Bobby Knight, his screaming, tantrums, chair throwing incidents, and how he embarrassed the United States during the Pan American Games in Puerto Rico by punching out a policeman. Someone told me there is still an open warrant for his arrest in Puerto Rico.

I used to ask Bob to assign me to just one Indiana basketball game so when I walked out on the floor I could be in charge. I told him when Knight came over to say "hello" or even shook hands, I would call a technical foul on him and throw him out of the game! Bob always responded, "Fred, you're trying to get me fired." I said, "He'll get you anyway." Eventually, before Knight was fired at Indiana, he did get Bob dismissed from his job.

Who's Calling? From Where?

Tommy Hensley and I had a Monday night football game in Miami and decided to take our wives to the game for a short vacation afterwards. We flew to the Bahamas on Tuesday morning. I still had to phone the league office as I did the morning following a game. I almost forgot, but did have a cellular phone with me. My wife, Dolores, Tommy and Johnny Belle Hensley and I were all standing on the dock in Paradise Island in our bathing suits as I was going through things with Art McNally. He kept going on and on and just wouldn't let me off the phone. Everyone was impatient and anxious to get the beach to relax.

I finally held the phone out to the waves and said, "Art, just listen to that surf. You're keeping me from those waves." I don't think he had any idea where I was and by the time we hung up, I also knew that he didn't appreciate my attitude. It was at least a year before the league office figured out that I was the one who made the collect call from the Bahamas.

I Have A Job For You

In the early 90s when Jerry Glanville, a heck of a guy, was coaching the Atlanta Falcons, yelled at me the entire game. He was screaming, "Fred, you're killing us. You're killing us," even if someone else made the call.

Finally he screams out, "By God you better have a job for me. You're costing me my job here because of your officiating." A few plays later when the action was on his sideline, I went over and said, "Coach, you won't believe this, but I do have a job for you . . . in the insurance business back in West Virginia. And, I'm serious. So, if anything happens to you here, call me because I do have a job for you." He looked at me, started laughing and then walked away.

I really did have a job for him. He is a super guy and would have been great in any kind of sales or marketing job.

The Missing Balls

It wasn't quite the incident of *The Caine Mutiny* and the missing strawberries, but the league office became concerned over footballs disappearing. We would get a bag of balls for each half. It was either 12 or 13. Our job was to get the balls back when the game was over but sometimes they were missing from the bag. When Art told me he had word that the previous week our crew had two balls missing, I said very surprised, "Art, it couldn't have been our crew. We had six balls missing." He didn't think it was very funny.

This Ball Is For Our Mascot

One time Art McNally brought his wife Sharon with him to San Francisco. As we were driving back to our hotel after the game, we thought we should do something for her that also would irritate Art. The best idea that we thought of that we knew Art would not like, was to give her a game ball. Art is in the front seat with her and Jerry got a game ball out of the bag. I said, "Sharon, on behalf of our crew, we want to name you our mascot and Jerry has something special to give you."

During all of this, Art began stuttering "You can't do that. You can't give her that ball." She wasn't buying any of this. She looked at the football and said," Look, Art, there's Pete Rozelle's autograph on the ball." Of course, the commissioner's autograph was stamped on every NFL football. Sharon was so excited that there wasn't much that Art could do. "You guys know you can't do that," he said. And I replied, "But she's our mascot and you should have done that for her." Now she's siding with us. When we got back to the hotel she was in the lobby for a couple of hours showing everybody her ball and telling them she is our mascot. Art went upstairs to his room. I don't know whether he allowed her to keep the ball, but most likely he did.

The Longest Flag Throw

Ed Marion was my headlinesman for a couple of years. He also was a very funny person and could get away with things with Art McNally that I couldn't. They both were from the Philadelphia area and worked together as officials for a number of years including high school and college games. We always speculated that Eddie had something he was holding over Art's head.

We're calling a Thanksgiving Day game in Detroit and all of a sudden he makes a call and throws the flag from one side of the field all the way across to the other side. When we're all in the dressing room after the game I look at Art and say, "Eddie broke the NFL record today for the longest throw of a flag on a penalty. But, you'll be happy to know that the record for a correct call is still intact." Eddie had thrown the flag across the field but missed the penalty. There wasn't any.

When he would tell jokes, the rest of us would get on his case, even when they were funny. We called him the seventh funniest person on our crew. Of course there were only seven. Art did think it was funny the way we would hammer Eddie about his jokes. The next year, however, Eddie was on a different crew. I think he asked Art to be moved.

Call Security!

The league office had a policy of wanting to know if any official was not on time for a pre-game meeting. We had a game in New Orleans and Eddie Marion was late. First of all, I would never have reported him or any member of my crew to the league office for being late. I would have taken care of it myself. If Art had heard it from someone else and called me about it, I would have said, "Art, I'm not going to give you that answer. You ask Eddie if he was late." I would have done this even if he would have fired me.

Well, when he came into the meeting we were watching a film. Before we started the film, a nice cleaning lady was getting the room in order and we were talking with her. She said she had never seen a professional football game so I told her "Sit right down at this table and you can help us grade the officials." She did right next to the projector.

When Eddie came in 20 minutes later, he sits right next to her and tries to get cute with her. She's not having any of it and looks at me and asks if he is part of our team. "Hey, I don't even know who this guy is, but I'll tell you that we don't want him in here," I responded. When she jumped up and started to get hotel security I had to stop her and tell her everything was all right.

Welcome to the Ship of the Damned

When Bob Wortman was first assigned to my crew, he wasn't happy about it. If you hadn't worked with Tommy Hensley and me and our crew, you had no way of knowing how serious we were about officiating and the kind of job we did on the field. The people that worked with us, loved us. We used to talk about having a waiting list. When people asked, we would tell them that we would put them on our wait list and let them know the first time we had an opening.

Once when Bob was moping around, Tommy and I presented him

with a T-shirt with "Welcome to the Ship of the Damned." That year Vince Jacobs, another member of our crew, had a heart attack. Bob used to look up at the sky and say, "I know he [Wyant] killed you because you were on his crew." We all laughed, of course, but weren't sure whether or not Bob was really joking.

We had that kind of relationship. During meetings we would say things and call each other names we didn't do on the field or traveling. In the meeting, the comedy was unbelievable and the language was worse that sailors on a boat. But it was all in love and comradeship. We just had a grand time.

We had a Monday night game and Bob filled in for an injured official, working with another crew on Sunday. When he came into our dressing room I asked him how he got along with the other crew and did he enjoy working with them. "That was the worst. It was so boring," he told us. "In the dressing room before the game I finally stood up and yelled at the top of my voice, 'Would someone please call me %*$#&%&$' and then sat down. I just missed all the things you used to say about me."

At the end of the season Bob was taken away from our crew. The league office would take a strong crew and put some of the guys on weaker crews. I could never understand why they wouldn't just keep making the strong crews even stronger. He was assigned to Red Cashion who is a delightful person and super official. But Bob wouldn't have any part of it. He wasn't happy and let the league know how he felt. They told him he was either going to officiate on Cashion's crew or not officiate at all.

During a pre-season game, his first experience with the new team, Red came up to him and said, "Bob, it doesn't look like you're happy here." And, Bob replied, "You're %*$&^(% right I'm not." But Bob, being the professional he is, ended up doing a great job working with Red Cashion. If he ever wants to be a referee, he'll certainly know how to say "Firrrrst Down!"

Beirut Here I Come

When the NFL expanded with an international league in Europe they first sent regular teams and officials' crews from the United States. I went to London twice for games. Now Europe is a training ground for players as well as young officials.

At one of our summer clinics, someone asked me if I had ever worked one of the American Bowls. I replied "Yes" and said "Art is sending me over there to work the first Lebanese Bowl. I'm excited about it. They are going to try and experiment for the first time with just one official." That got a big laugh and of course Lebanon was a war zone disaster at the time. Everyone thought that was funny.

Meeting Celebrities

When you're flying coast-to-coast and especially at night you run into a lot of celebrities. I took a number of "red-eye" flights back from the West Coast. One night I met Anthony Quinn. Another time I met Buck Owens and all of the cast of *Hee Haw*.

Another time, in the TWA Ambassador's lounge in the St. Louis airport, I saw Jimmy Stewart sitting with his wife. As I got ready to leave to board my flight, I walked over and introduced myself and told him how much I admired him and enjoyed his movies. He thanked me, was most gracious and introduced me to his wife.

One of the most memorable times was meeting Chubby Checker on a flight. I had met him once before but he had no idea who I was. He was in the window seat in the last row of first class. I walked up to him and said, "Chubby, Fred Wyant." He said, "Fred, how super to see you." And I introduced him to all of the members of my crew. On that same plan there were three professional baseball umpires, Marty "Hello 'Dere" Allen and Gordon Lightfoot and his group. I spent most of the trip in the back talking with Lightfoot who was just a super nice guy.

One time, coming out of Morgantown, Tiny Tim, who used to sing "Tiptoe Through the Tulips" on his ukelele, was on the same flight. I also met Dionne Warwick and Jim Nabors in Los Angeles. There were always a lot of movie stars at the Rams' games.

Ricardo Montalban was doing a play in Pittsburgh and staying at our hotel. He was alone in the lounge and I and several members of my crew went over, introduced ourselves and invited him to join us for dinner. He accepted and was absolutely delightful. I remember he had a huge cigar. Al Sabato, a member of our crew, arrived late and was stupefied when he sat down to join us. He started conversing in Italian with Montalban, who speaks Spanish. It turned out to be a really nice evening. He was a real gentleman. Al got his home telephone number and told him he would leave complimentary tickets for him whenever our crew was in Los Angeles.

Going Through Weather Like the Mailman

Morgantown, Pittsburgh and Buffalo do not always have the friendliest environment for airline travel. I left Morgantown for Buffalo and was connecting with a flight in Pittsburgh on a Saturday. When I checked in at the Pittsburgh counter I was told all flights were canceled because of four feet of snow in Buffalo. They also said there would be no Saturday flights but there might be a possibility for Sunday. It wasn't snowing in either Morgantown or Pittsburgh.

I got back on a plane for Morgantown, went to a little Mexican restaurant for dinner and called Art. I had tried to reach him earlier when I was in Pittsburgh, but he was at the Army-Navy game in Philadelphia. When he found out I was back in Morgantown he was livid. He told me to get back there and demand to get on a plane because I was in the NFL. I told him, "Art, I've never big timed anybody in my life and I'm not going to start now. If you want me on a plane, then you should call and get me on a plane."

He continued on and on about what I should have done. I asked him if his wife was running the officiating crews on Saturday afternoon during all of the terrible storms in the Northeast when he was at a college football game. "I couldn't reach you to talk about what we needed to do," I told him. He decided to send someone else to Buffalo to be the referee or an extra official.

Sunday morning I was able to get a flight to Buffalo. When I got into the cab to go to the stadium, I began changing clothes. You could hardly even see the lanes of traffic, the snowdrifts three-to-four-feet above the roof of the car and here I was stripping to put on my uniform.

I got to the dressing room about seven minutes before kickoff. Fred Swearington was going over things with the crew. I had been on his crew when he was a referee, he was on my crew when I was a referee. We were friends. I said, "Okay, Fred, thanks a lot. I'll take it from here." We waked out and officiated the game and went home. The alternate didn't get into that game.

Here was another conflict I had with the league front office. I managed the situation and took care of it.

You Must Pay Attention In Class

One thing about our crew was the fact we were always doing something different. We were getting prepared for a game in Pittsburgh and Jimmy Rosser, who was in his second year in the league and on my crew, was sitting in the back of a room beside a window. Art caught him looking out the window and jumped all over him. During a break, we had to have a test on the rules. I put something together and handed it to Jimmy. It went something like this: "Jimmy, while you were looking out the window, how many black cars were driving north in the last five minutes and how many were going south? What was the total number of cars you saw and the total number of buses? Everyone broke out laughing, including Jimmy, although he was embarrassed about how many cars were out there.

The Joke Is On You Adrian

One of my deep officials was Adrian Burke, the former Philadelphia Eagles quarterback and a Houston attorney. He still holds the NFL record for most touchdown passes in a game with seven along with Sid

Luckman, George Blanda, Y.A. Tittle and Joe Kapp. We were staying at the Essex House in New York City preparing for a Giants game. It turns out another crew also was in the hotel preparing for a Jets game on Monday night.

We were getting ready to review our game film and invited the other crew to join us. I told them to go along with me with whatever I do and to agree with me. They all had a critique sheet which we had every week. Adrian was the last to arrive for the meeting not knowing what I had in store for him.

We were critiquing the game as we went through the film. Then there was a deep pass pattern near Adrian. A receiver came down and made a cut and the defender was there. If they were within two inches of each other, I would be surprised. As soon as they were almost in contact with each other, I said, "Holy, Toledo, how could you let that go, Adrian?" He said, "What do you mean? What do you mean?" We reversed the film and replayed it. Looking at it again, he said, "I didn't see anything on that."

So, we re-ran it again and when the receiver made the cut, I said, "Geemanee Christmas, no wonder we're in trouble. You've got to make those calls, Adrian." Adrian, of course, had no problem making tough calls. He was the key man in the famous immaculate reception verdict for Pittsburgh against Oakland.

In the room we had a dozen or more officials agreeing with me and he starts to go crazy. "There's nothing there. You're not serious. Run that back," he kept saying. And we kept running the play over and over. Of course there was absolutely nothing to call but everyone got a huge laugh out of it.

On a serious side, it does point out that if a group of guys like those in the supervisor's office disagreed with our crew, our 7-0 decision on a call could be called a mistake and we would all be penalized for it.

Where Is Don Ho When You Need Him?

I was assigned to referee the annual Pro Hall of Fame game in Canton, Ohio. The pre-game meal was in a hospitality tent for all of the VIPs, media and others. I arrived wearing a brown and white Hawaiian puka shell necklace. My crew included Frank Sinkovich and Stan Javie. Nick Skorich and Jack Reader were there from the league office as observers. Everybody was in on the joke but Reader.

The other officials started the joke by saying: "You're not going to let him wear those beads are you?" They added that I looked like some kind of fruitcake. This is before the days of pierced ears or pierced anything. Just wearing the necklace was considered radical.

Jack being the diplomat he is said: "Fred, are you planning to wear those during the game?" I said: "Well, Jack, yes I am. It has to do with my religion in West Virginia." He questioned, "Oh, your religion?" "It's the church I belong to in West Virginia," I added.

He then asked, "Do you have to wear those puka beads all the time?" He was Catholic, so I asked him about the medal he was wearing, "Do you wear it all the time." And he said, "Yeah, all the time." I said, "Jack, well, it's the same thing. It's a new religion in West Virginia, and that's what we wear–puka shells."

By this time Stan and Frank are going crazy and really giving it to him. "I am not working this game, Jack," said Stan. "You get him to get them off." Sinky agreed with him. Then Nick Skorich added "You are going to have to do something about that. You are going to have to handle it."

Before we went on the field, I looked at him and said, "Do you want to wear the necklace?" He looked at me and everyone in the place started laughing. Jack had really been taken advantage of. He was a good sport and laughed about it. He also was from the league office and I'm sure the story got back to everyone there. But, that's what fun is all about. If you're not having fun in life, don't do it.

Where's the Coach?

One of my most embarrassing moments as a referee was in 1976 when I had a New York Jets game. Early in the game I had to give a notice to the coaches and I walked over to the sidelines and asked, "Where's the coach?" I knew Lou Holtz was the Jets' coach, but I had never met him. While I was looking for someone I thought would be the coach, this little guy with thick glasses and a hat pulled down over head and wearing khakis came up and began mumbling something to me. I had a message to deliver to the coach and I didn't want to be interrupted by anyone, so I pushed him aside and yelled out "Where's the coach?" The same slight individual came up to me again and as I started to push him away a second time, Joe Namath looks at me, points at Lou Holtz and says, "Fred, he *is* the coach!" Oh, was I ever embarrassed!

I learned later that he was a fellow Mountaineer from Follansbee, West Virginia. Had I known that before the game, I would have made a point of introducing myself. Since then I have closely followed his most successful career. I've since learned that he also followed the WVU teams of my time.

Of course, who would have thought someone only 5'10" and weighing 150 pounds, wearing thick glasses and with a lisp problem would be a football coach anywhere, much less in the NFL? I've never stereotyped anyone since. Lou's record certainly proves that!

> *Someone left my name off the list the day God handed out physiques. I have the imposing, muscular body of a malnutrition poster boy. I don't look like a coach and wish Fred had made up for not recognizing me during the game!–*
> Lou Holtz

Art Taught Me Everything I Know!

My crew and I were driving back to our hotel in New York City after a night game in Giants Stadium in New Jersey. Art McNally was riding with us and he was in the back seat of a large station wagon with two members of my crew. One was a rookie and the other was in his second year. Both were trying to make conversation with Art but he is not the easiest person to talk to.

As one of them started to ask him, "We understand that Fred began his officiating in the NFL on your crew and . . . " Art's voice jumped up 14 octaves. "Don't blame me for the way he turned out," Art said. Everybody really laughed at that, but I believe Art was serious and didn't want to take any responsibility for me.

CHAPTER XI

Where Do We Go from Here?

Paul Tagliabue has one of the toughest jobs in sports. He succeeded Pete Rozelle as commissioner of the NFL. Rozelle, considered by many to be the greatest commissioner in all of sports, served the league over three decades from 1960 until he retired in 1989.

Rozelle was an innovator. Tagliabue is a lawyer. Rozelle was a marketing genius. Tagliabue is a lawyer. Rozelle recognized the power of television in building the growth of the sport. Tagliabue is a lawyer. Rozelle was an outstanding public relations professional. Tagliabue is a lawyer. Rozelle was personable, outgoing and truly a people person. Tagliabue is a lawyer.

While professional football had been played in the United States for more than 40 years, it was under Rozelle's leadership that it became the country's most popular sport. During his reign as commissioner, probably also the longest tenure in any sport, the league went through an evolution and revolution. Some of professional football's highlights under Rozelle's leadership included creating the first playoff bowl; the Super Bowl; Monday night television; mega-million dollar television contracts; moving the NFL's offices from Philadelphia to New York City; expansion with new teams; founding NFL Properties; helping dedicate the Pro Football Hall of Fame in Canton; establishing NFL Films; adding one sudden-death overtime period for preseason and regular-season games; moving the kickoffs from the 40-yard line back to the 35-yard line; and returning the ball to the point of scrimmage rather than the 20-yard line after a missed field goal attempt.

In 1986, the NBC telecast of Super Bowl XX topped the final episode of M*A*S*H as the most-viewed television program in history with an audience of 127 million viewers. More than 70 percent of American television sets were tuned into watch Chicago beat New England 46-10. The game was televised to 59 countries throughout the world and an estimated 300 million Chinese viewed a tape delay of the game in March.

As television exposure increased, so did fans buying tickets to go to games. At the end of every season, the league reported paid attendance throughout the league was the highest in history.

There were a number of other changes that included increasing the number of officials on a crew from five to seven and changing rules to add action and tempo to the games. Rules also were revised to emphasize additional player safety such as moving the goal posts from the goal line to the end zone, prohibiting players from blocking below the waist during kickoffs, punts and field goal attempts and wearing torn or altered equipment and exposed pads that could be dangerous, instructing officials to quickly whistle a play dead when a quarterback was clearly in the grasp of a tackler and placing greater restrictions on contact in the area of the head, neck and face.

The leadership of the game has changed tremendously. Gone are leaders like Bert Bell, George Halas, Vince Lombardi, Tom Landry, Art Rooney, Tex Schramm, and George Preston Marshall. Don Shula, one of the driving forces in many of the rules changes, is now retired and about the only owner from the "old guard" is Wellington Mara of the Giants.

Pete Rozelle was the right commissioner at the right time. Perhaps with the new ownership in the league today its image when of some of its superstars have problems with drugs, alcohol and sexual abuse, as well as owners wanting to break contracts with cities over leases as municipal stadiums, franchise moves, labor and antitrust cases, age discrimination suits and EEOC complaints, a lawyer like Paul Tagliabue should be the commissioner. Unfortunately, today we live in an overly-litigious society. One thing about Rozelle, however, was that he would always hire the best professional needed to do the job and he remained the man in charge.

> *The NFL's leadership has changed. Older coaches wouldn't take anything from the players. In those days, if you broke the rules, you would be gone. Today, coaches and owners stick up for their good ball players. It's a different game.*–
> Ben Dreith

Rozelle in fact did bring in Tagliabue, a former captain of Georgetown's basketball team, as counsel to the league in 1969. He wanted help during the Joe Namath-Bachelors III incident when the former Jets quarterback threatened to retire prior to the '69 season rather than adhere to the commissioner's requirement that Namath sell his interest in the New York nightspot. When elected commissioner, Tagliabue was a partner at Covington & Burling, a Washington, D.C. law firm, and the league's principal outside counsel.

Money and greed seem to be the motivation and driving force for owners today. Not only are so many of the players the stereotypes of the role Cuba Gooding, Jr. played in the movie, *Jerry Maguire*, but I hear owners screaming out: "Show me the money!"

> *There are no sportsmen as owners in the league today. They are all businessmen. The Rooneys, Maras and others were all sportsmen. The game has gotten to be where I don't enjoy it anymore.*–Charley Sumner

There are second generations of leadership now in the NFL. Sons are continuing the legacy of their fathers. One such leader is Dan Rooney, president of the Pittsburgh Steelers. He worked in every area of the organization since graduating from Duquesne University in 1955. The Rooney family not only is an institution in professional football, it is in Pittsburgh where all of the Rooneys are leaders and benefactors to the community. Dan, in fact, is one of the city's most involved executives in civic affairs. You never hear him threatening the people in Western Pennsylvania about moving the Steelers out of Pittsburgh unless the team is given certain favors. He also is very active on a number of league committees.

His father, Art Rooney, who was inducted into the Pro Football Hall of Fame in 1964, founded the team in 1933 as the Pittsburgh Pirates. The name was changed to Steelers in 1945. The Steelers have always been a Rooney family business. It is the fifth-oldest franchise in the NFL behind the Chicago (now Arizona) Cardinals, Green Bay Packers, Chicago Bears and New York Giants.

> *I knew Fred when he was playing for West Virginia University and I was at Duquesne. I recruited him and recommended him to be an official in this league and saw him advance to become a referee. He is a very able guy.*–
> Daniel M. Rooney

Another such leader carrying on the role of his father, the legendary Paul Brown, is Michael Brown of the Cincinnati Bengals. So many athletes leave college without a degree and assume football will provide them with everything they need in life. This is terribly wrong. Colleges have failed when they send athletes out from the security of a campus world into the real world. Some NFL coaches and teams put tremendous pressure on their players to be working at the game year round. Michael Brown knows, as his father did, that football is not everything, but only a stepping stone to the future and life after football.

Michael Brown's father also is in the Pro Football Hall of Fame and was inducted in 1967. He was responsible for building the Browns dynasty in Cleveland with a record of 167-53-8. He coached Cleveland from 1946-49 to four AAFC titles and to three NFL championships from 1950-62. After six years of retirement he returned to coaching in 1968 until 1975 with the Cincinnati Bengals.

I finished my college playing career the fall of 1955 and the spring of 1956 was ready to go out in the real world. I was self-employed, looking forward to playing with the Washington Redskins and thought that maybe I really didn't need a degree. When I was really successful in my business, I realized maybe I didn't need a degree, but I wanted my degree.

> *My father believed the players should work in the off-season to get their degrees or to get out in the throes of a real job. They needed to prepare for life after football. I don't think that has changed today. In only recent years have we seen a tick up in scholastic levels of the players. There was a time when some players came out of college and could barely read. These were exceptions, but they did exist. Players now make more money and their lives after football should be the best. Our team does not emphasize off-season workouts or other activities that restrict the players chances of going to school or getting started in another career. We want to see them do things other than football.–*Michael Brown

August 15, 1975 is one of the proudest days of my life. I finished work on my degree from West Virginia University. I went to the ceremony the following spring, wore a cap and gown, and had my whole family there to celebrate with me. It was one of the most memorable times in my life. I didn't realize how important having the degree is to me.

A good friend of mine also believes it is never too late to get a college degree. Hot Rod Hundley was one of the greatest basketball players in West Virginia University's history. He finished his college career in 1957, was the #1 draft choice of the NBA and played five years with the Minneapolis and later Los Angeles Lakers. He played on the West team in the NBA's All-Star game several times. At the Lakers, he teamed with a couple of other Mountaineers–Jerry West and coach Fred Schaus and for a couple of seasons, Bobby Joe Smith.

Rod has become a successful entrepreneur, in-demand speaker and radio and television personality. Since the Utah Jazz came into the National Basketball Association as the New Orleans Jazz, Rod has been the team's radio and television announcer. He also has been picked by networks for college games and special events. He is in demand as an entertaining speaker. You might say he has it all. But he hadn't completed work on his degree and hadn't taken a college class in more than 40 years.

He decided he wanted his degree and made arrangements with the university to take classes during his off-season to complete his requirements. On May 14, 2000, at the age of 65, Hot Rod, in full cap and gown, walked across the stage to get his degree. His effort was self-motivated. Other athletes need to be motivated and it is the responsibility of our college coaches and professional teams and the leagues to insure this happens. A multi-million dollar contract or bonus is not what life is all about.

A *Time* magazine article last year talked about how the American public was getting disgusted with the dire state of major league sports and spoiled, overpaid professional athletes. But what really told the true story was the letter-to-the-editor that fans wrote about the article. Here is what Gordon Held of Young Harris, Georgia wrote: " . . . We are fools to spend our time watching a bunch of spoiled, overpaid athletes. These people are the farthest thing from the role models we would like for our children and have been known for poor sportsmanship, drug abuse, sexual offenses and insatiable greed."

Other writers suggested the ticket-buying fans exacerbated the problem and if they stopped spending money on tickets, merchandising and junk food and playing sports rather than watching them, the problem would disappear. And some suggested supporting college and high school sports. Four season tickets to a Division II college cost $150 a year with parking 50 yards from the gate.

Show Me the Stadium

Typical of the greed today is the threats new owners hold over mayors, city councils and fans, demanding that news stadiums be built, maintained and refurbished and with luxury boxes so the owners can charge large corporations thousands upon thousands of dollars for the right to watch a game. Owners are literally blackmailing communities into building and developing new stadiums with most of the risk and none of the profits and guarantees for the future being given to the communities.

Being a businessman my entire life, I often wonder when I look at these proposed arrangements why, if a community is to foot the bill, why then don't they receive part ownership so they can share and reap the benefits of their efforts? Otherwise owners would not spend so much time telling the public that the team can no longer play in their city because it doesn't have the type of facility that will allow them to reap large amounts of profits during their ownership stint.

A great example is in Cleveland where the fan support has always been unbelievable. Even though the stadium was older, it seated around 80,000 people and was always packed to the brim with Cleveland Browns fans every home game. In February 1994, Art Modell, owner of the Browns, said the team would never leave Cleveland as long as he owned the team. At the end of the 1995 season they moved to Baltimore and became the Ravens, replacing the Colts who moved in the middle of the night to Indianapolis. Remember the Rams? They started in Cleveland, moved to Los Angeles, were still called the Los Angeles Rams when they were in Anaheim and now are in St. Louis. Where does Georgia Frontiere want to live next?

The only other business organization that never has to be accountable to the public is government, regardless of the level. The tobacco industry is heavily subsidized by the federal government, almost as much as members of Congress are subsidized by the tobacco interests. Now owners want to be treated like the tobacco industry and have decided that they are in such an enviable position that they can not act like federal, state and local governments and have their cake and own the club and make all the profit.

Any politician who advocates spending public money for a new stadium should read several books on the subject: *Field of Schemes: How the Great Stadium Swindle Turns Public Money into Private Profit*, by Joanna Cagan and Neil deMause; *Major League Losers: The Real Cost of Sports and Who's Paying for It* by Mark S. Rosentraub; *Home Team: Professional Sports and the American Metropolis* by Michael N.

Danielson, and *Sports, Jobs and Taxes: The Economic Impact of Sports Teams and Stadium* by Roger G. Noll and Andrew Zimbalist.

Cagan and deMause point out that owners of sports teams exaggerate the economic benefits of a stadium to threatening to relocate the team if one isn't built. They expose some of the deepest current urban conspiracies between newspaper owners, local politicians and real estate developers.

Noll and Zimbalist have case studies of the new stadiums in Baltimore, Chicago, Cincinnati, Cleveland, Indianapolis, San Francisco and Minneapolis-St. Paul. They conclude that the magnitude of the net subsidy exceeds the financial benefit of a new stadium, that sports teams and facilities are not a source of local economic growth and employment and the reason most cities subsidize sports teams is because of the intense popularity among voters and businesses. The teams do not pay for themselves with increased tax revenues, local economic development and job creation. Both authors are econ professors–Noll at Stanford and Zimbalist at Smith.

In *Home Team*, Danielson looks at the political aspects of connections between professional sports teams and cities and notes the increasing competition to provide lavish publicly funded facilities for private business ventures.

Rosentraub, who is director of the Center for Urban Policy and the Environment at Indiana University writes that the taxpayers are forced to shell out millions of dollars to subsidize the expenses of wealth owners of professional teams. He notes that owners blackmail cities into huge subsidies. One reviewer of *Major League Losers* wrote that the book is a must read for every New Yorker, especially Mayor Rudolph Giuliani.

When New York Yankees owner George Steinbrenner wanted a new billion-dollar-plus stadium for his baseball team, he virtually had a deal put together with the Mayor Giuliani. The two of them even had a site selected on Manhattan's upper west side. Then some city council members got together with a coalition of taxpayers who insisted it be put it to a public vote. What was so bad about "The House that Ruth Built?" Giuliani was outraged that the people wanted to vote. "They will vote against it. Vote it down. They don't know what they are doing," said the mayor. Really, isn't that what democracy is all about? Giuliani needs a remedial course in Government 101.

Judge Douglas McKeon of the Bronx ruled that the question of moving the Yankees to a new stadium is an emotional one and that every New Yorker should have a say. An angry Giuliani called the judge "the product of a Democratic machine" who gave "a Democratic answer, not an honest answer." Unfortunately, he was overruled in a state appeals court that said a commission established by the mayor to propose changes in the city charter is operating legally and the stadium question could not go on the ballot for the taxpayers to decide whether or not they wanted to subsidize Steinbrenner.

When profits are not enough, then the howl goes up to get a new facility, to get more concessions, luxury boxes, or the team will move. Way down at the bottom of the owners' priority list are the American families who have made professional sports what they are today. The average American family is left out. The typical working father or mother can no longer afford to take their kids to a professional game. They don't have $250 to spend on an afternoon to watch many players, who don't want to be role models, compete for owners who couldn't care less whether John Q. Public and the family get any breaks whatsoever.

In the end, who really supports professional teams? It is the public. John Q. Public. The typical American family. If they don't come to the game or don't watch it on television, then there are no professional teams, multi-million dollar paid and pampered players, there is no need for luxury boxes, and there is no need for $5 hot dogs. What is the solution?

1. Cities, counties and states need to demand a piece of the ownership if they are going to foot the entire bill for new facilities. A poll by The Washington Post found that 72 percent of Marylanders opposed using tax dollars to build football stadiums for the Washington Redskins and Baltimore Ravens. Similar opposition has surfaced in several cities. The late Jack Kent Cooke did put up his own money to build a new stadium for the Redskins.

The taxpayers in Maryland weren't as lucky. The 69,000-seat stadium for the Ravens cost $220 million. The team did contribute $20 million—only 10 percent—but 10 percent more than most other teams want to do in their cities. That allows them to play there, rent free, for 30 years. The bulk of the money was raised through the sale of revenue bonds backed by the state and a sports lottery, expected to contribute $32 million a year to pay off the bonds. They also expect to sell the commercial naming rights to the stadium for as much as $50 million.

Yet the market for new stadiums and arenas is booming. There are plans for 50 new facilities for baseball, basketball, football and ice hockey being seriously considered or under construction in the U.S. Even the most modest of facilities will cost $100 million. The taxpayer gets stuck holding the tab for billions of dollars of infrastructure expenses for professional teams.

The Washington state legislature adopted a $300 million package of public financing for a new stadium for the Seattle Mariners under threats that the team would leave the city. This use of public money to support private enterprise is done under the guise of economic development. The biggest problem with such corporate giveaways is that it is done by cities least able to afford them. Urban taxpayers already suffer an increasing and very high tax burden.

Professional sports teams do provide a great sense of civic pride, especially if the team is a winner and brings home a world championship every now and then. But should the taxpayers provide this kind of support for multi-millionaire owners and athletes when they show loyalty for the fans that make it possible? I think not.

Robert Baade, a professor at Lake Forest College in Lake Forest, Illinois, has done studies looking at stadiums and city economics in 48 major U.S. cities. He found no relationship between stadium projects and higher economic growth. He writes: "After a thorough examination of an unprecedented quantity of data related to professional sports and host area per capita personal income, there is no factual basis for the conventional argument that professional sports stadiums and teams have a significant impact on a region's economic growth." He also believes that the professional sports industry is relatively small and cities should be wary of committing substantial portions of their capital budgets to building stadiums and otherwise subsidizing professional sports in the expectation of substantial income and job growth. Dr. Baade adds that "As a catalyst for economic development, professional sports' batting average fails to quality as big league."

It is hard to argue this with politicians who vote for the subsidies because they are guaranteed free tickets to any event they want to attend at the new stadium or arena with their families and friends.

The Detroit Lions signed an agreement with the city to make them residents of their new downtown stadium for at least 35 years. They agreed to pay $5 million to $8 million a year for operating costs, $250,000 a year for maintenance, pay for all capital improvements and pick up the tab for 5,000 tickets a year that will be issued to youngsters from low-income families.

Where are the Raiders? In Oakland? Or in Los Angeles? The way they keep moving around California it could Anaheim, Azuza or Cucamonga next. The team has given only grief to the community in Oakland by blocking a restructuring plan designed to remedy the scheme of paying back public funds used to refurbish the stadium through the sales of personal seat licenses. The Raiders planned to sell the licenses between $250 and $4,000, good through the year 2005, for the right to buy season tickets. Considerably fewer than 55,000 originally expected fans signed up for the plan. The city has sued the Raiders, the Raiders have countersued, and there is much unhappiness in Raiderland.

Why would Al Davis get upset because the city wants guarantees? The rent was to increase from $525,000 to $1.025 million over the next three years. Or to allow the stadium to be named UMAX Coliseum after a high-tech firm that was willing to pay $1.5 million a year for 10 years to see and promote its name on the stadium. Davis now has to deal with a new mayor–former California governor Jerry Brown who is known for being frugal.

There has to be a move back to reality. Perhaps local ownership of the team, such as with the Packers in Green Bay, is the only way.

2. The NFL needs to do a better job of screening the ownership groups that are now buying franchises. If you are going to talk about big money then they need to be the type of entrepreneurial owners such as Jack Kent Cooke, who built his own arena outside of Washington, D.C., and previously built The Forum in Inglewood, California, after fighting with the tri-party city, state and county governments of Los Angeles over dates at the sports arena. Another entrepreneur was Walter O'Mally who built Dodger Stadium in Los Angeles.

Now if the new management of the Redskins or Dodgers want to move, they have no obligation to the local community. But if the community puts up the money, then the public should have some say if and when a team can move, and what they are going to charge the public for tickets, concessions and parking.

Green Bay has survived very nicely. There is a great community spirit. They don't even have a covered stadium. When it snows, the players play in the snow and the fans protect themselves from adverse weather conditions. What is best for the American public? The Green Bay Packers? Or the Cleveland to Los Angeles to Anaheim to St. Louis Rams? Or the Oakland to Los Angeles to Oakland to wherever Raiders? Or lying to the public that you will always keep a team in that city? I would vote for Green Bay.

3. The owners should designate one or more games every year to give to the public in a community the right to buy tickets for a game at considerably reduced prices so children can attend. They are the future success for the NFL and need to be treated as such. For these games the concession stand prices should be reasonable. These young people should get a taste of something their grandparents and great grandparents got when they were growing up. This has all but disappeared from them and their parents.

4. There needs to be more innovation like what was done in Philadelphia by putting a judge and court inside the stadium to deal with unruly fans. There needs to be policing of the tailgate parties which have become a drinking party with a little eating. Fans at athletic contests have the right to go to the game, yell for the team they choose, but they do not have to be abused by other fans or hear profanity. Ownership needs to take leadership and the Eagles and Philly's Mayor Ed Rendell have set a great example for others to follow.

Where Is the Leadership for New Officials?

The great majority of football officials don't give up their weekends or evenings to officiate a game because they want to or because they believe one day they will be able to get into the NFL. Some do it because they are community-minded. Others are former athletes who want to continue to keep their hand in the game. And there are others who want to be involved with the sport but didn't have an opportunity to play when in high school or college, for whatever reason. In today's economy it may be a way for some individuals to earn additional income. There certainly is nothing wrong with that.

Many find that being an official, regardless of the level of the game–Pop Warner or flag league to organized conferences at junior high schools and high schools to colleges and universities–is a way to provide something to the community. It also means hard work and the desire to build a reputation as a fine football official or an outstanding football official, to being the very best official in the league, state or conference.

These officials need to take as much interest in the rules and mechanics of the game as an official in the NFL. But the concept of having professional officials officiating on a Pop Warner level, of course, is unrealistic. I've seen excellent officiating at high school football games. I've seen calls made that were outstanding, but were not considered to be so by the fans. I see the same intense effort by these high school officials as is seen on a professional level.

When I started officiating I began at the high school level. Today, an individual with aspirations of being a college or even NFL official, probably will have to start in the pee wee, Pop Warner, college intramural and high school jayvee leagues and then move to high school, small colleges and large colleges before having a chance to be considered a candidate for the NFL.

I imagine the odds of somebody starting off with their goal to be an NFL referee, as I did, would be as great as a youngster today wanting to play in the NFL, NBA or Major League Baseball. The odds are probably about the same for winning the lottery.

As officials decide to move up from one level to another, there needs to be more professionalism added to their thought on how they do the game. They need to study the rules more, have greater knowledge of the game, a better understanding of judgment, and continued observation of good sportsmanship. By the time one reaches the high school level, he probably is being supervised by one of the local area college officials who also has taken on an additional job of supervising and observing high school officials. There are some very talented people officiating high school football games who only want to do high school games.

My rookie year as a referee, when I went to our summer clinic, Fred really helped me. We visited the Steelers camp and he took me aside and said, 'Let's watch the linemen and see what holding is and isn't.' No one else made a gesture like that, but Fred did. He really helped me as an official and it had been a number of years since I had officiated a game as a referee. I was a line judge for three years and a deep man and you look at the game from a different perspective. Downfield, you're not involved with holding by interior lineman.–Dick Hantack

For an official to move to the next level he has to have help in the way of a tutor or mentor. When I first started, I was very fortunate in having the opportunity to work with the outstanding officials of that time in West Virginia. They were extremely helpful to me in developing my game. Sometimes people don't realize the pride that officials have in their game and how professional they are regardless of the level of competition.

My Only Game As An Umpire

I had just refereed the Florida State-Virginia Tech football game on Saturday and was scheduled to work the traditional Thanksgiving Day high school game between East Fairmont High School and West Fairmont High School. On our team was Hank Mazza, one of the best known and most seasoned and experienced referees in the state. I was in my eighth year, all as a referee, and three at the major college level. The conference did not assign officials by position. Hank, as the senior official, came to me and asked me what position I wanted to work. In respect for his years as a high school official, I said I didn't care. He then said, "I'd better ref this game. It will be a tough one." He then looked right and left and said, "I want you to be my umpire. And, I don't let everyone be my umpire."

I worked the entire game with enthusiasm and did so because of who he was and the fact I appreciated all the things he and others did for me as I was getting started. There was no way I was going to step up and tell him I'm now a big college referee. And there was no way Hank thought I was any better a referee than he was. That was the first, last and only time I have ever worked as an umpire.

Developing Professionalism

For there to be good officiating at all levels of competition, veteran officials have to take interest in the younger officials and help them move to higher levels. I've always had a rule that if a young official came to me and asked if I would recommend him to the next level, generally from high school to college or from college to the NFL, that I wanted to review film or tape of one or more of their games. I also would ask for their game schedule and do my best to see them officiate during their season.

I had schooling from masters for seven years. Officials coming into the league today don't have that same experience with veteran referees.–Jim Tunney

I told each that if I thought he was good enough to move to the next level, that I would call, write or otherwise recommend or refer him to the appropriate people in charge of that conference or level of competition. On the other hand, if I thought he needed more work, I would take the time to share with him what I thought they needed to do to improve his game. I would tell him when he felt he could do the things I wanted him to do to improve his game, then to call me so I could schedule a time to watch him work a game. I would repeat this procedure over again and again.

During my career I was very fortunate. I was exposed to and worked with the greatest officials in this sport. There are many who enjoyed the reputation of being the best in their time and the best of all time. I always appreciated the opportunity to be associated with them.

My philosophy was that I will seek and select those officials I felt most comfortable with and I would allow myself and my crew to do the best possible job even though we may not be recognized by the league office as being the best there is at that point in time.

Things changed considerably when Jerry Seeman took over from Art McNally in 1991. Seeman had been a former referee in the league and was business manager of a school system in Minnesota which qualified him to run a business. One thing he did know was that when he started to look at the officials in the league there were many he could not scare or control. These were people like me who had a mind of their own and didn't mind saying so when we felt we had something to say. This is the way great managers and leaders create success in any endeavor in life and business.

The quality of officiating in the NFL has deteriorated since Art McNally left–Jerry Bergman

From 1991 through 1997, 54 officials left the league either at his request or their own choice. The league only had 112 officials assigned in 16 crews. This was a tremendous turnover, losing that many senior officials, and their replacements coming in with absolutely no experience in the NFL. In 1998, nine officials retired who had combined experience of 177 years. Seeman's roster had only nine 20-year officials compared with McNally's 16 in his final year, 1990.

> *This level of turnover obviously has potential problems. Although there may be idiosyncracies to the industry that make it less problematic than in others.*–Dr. Leonard Biermann, professor of management, Texas A&M University
> *As good as an official is, it takes four to five years to 'become' an NFL official and to get the feel of the game. The league was left with 40 or more officials with less than five years of experience.*–Jim Tunney

By comparison, Major League Baseball has 68 umpires on its staff and has very little turnover, and zero in some years. At least until 1999 when 57 umpires resigned in an attempt to force a new labor contract. In the end, 25 withdrew their resignations but 22 were completely shocked to find themselves out of a six-figure job. The National Basketball Association has 58 referees and averages a turnover of only one or two a year.

Once, the "unofficial" word was that the maximum age for an NFL official was to be 59 years. No one 60 or older should be on the field working a game. This precipitated a number of lawsuits and complaints to the Equal Opportunities Employment Commission for age discrimination. Many of those who recently retired were in their 60s.

The "official" way Seeman's office handled the matter was to tell someone like me that if I didn't get a playoff game that year, my contract would not be renewed the following year. And who do you guess decided on which officials got playoff games? Not a difficult question. Of course, it was Seeman's office. This was a subtle method that they hoped would not create legal problems because of age or race or lack of firing procedures.

It was absolutely amazing how officials who had been given the word would all of a sudden end up with mistakes in a game that were irreversible, regardless of how many people on the crew believed that the league supervisors made the mistake. When the season was over, the official was then given the opportunity of either retiring or being told he would be "fired" by not having a new contract.

If you've never been fired before, it is a somewhat unnerving situation. Even if you are given the opportunity to retire instead of being fired, it still is an unnerving situation. Most of the officials in this category just quietly retired rather than be fired. But what is the difference? If the owners aren't concerned, the coaches and players should be concerned about the proficiency of officiating in the league with the turnover and loss of its most senior and experience officials.

Has the officiating improved since Jerry Seeman began forcing out older, experienced officials and requiring various runs, sprints and races and a stringent exercise and conditioning program? In my opinion, professionally speaking, I don't believe so. What he couldn't devise was a means of determining judgement, which is what it is all about during a game.

I understand that Seeman's philosophy is that every game is a Super Bowl and that is the way the officials must call the game. In addition to forcing the senior, most experienced to retire, he has fined and suspended officials. Gordon McCarter was fined $4,009 when his crew missed 12 men being on the field. And this was compounded when Steelers coach Bill Cowher was photographed shoving a photograph of the violation in McCarter's pocket. Umpire Chad Brown was fined $3,500 for writing a book about his NFL experiences.

Jerry Bergman was fined $2,000 for asking Green Bay quarterback Brett Favre for an autograph. And officials and others associated with the league have been obtaining autographs from the superstars for years without any incident. I don't know what he was trying to prove or the point he was trying to make, but it certainly was not a decision that would ever be a team building effort or morale booster. Some baseball umpires may be under scrutiny for being in the business of selling autographed baseballs.

> *Seeman was my head linesman his rookie year. He used shoestrings to tie his shirt to keep it from coming out of his pants and now wants everyone to do that. He would be so uptight he wouldn't even let anyone turn on the car radio when we were driving to the stadium. He demands every game be officiated like a Super Bowl. There is no difference. I've refereed the Super Bowl and work it no differently than any other game. Or any other game differently than I would if it were the Super Bowl. You always do the same throughout the season.* –Ben Dreith

I don't want to be critical of any of the new officials because I think if they had an opportunity to have been integrated with the officials that I worked with they would have had an opportunity to grow into independently strong football officials. I do hear from friends still "on the inside" that no one is having fun anymore. Not one friend of mine in the league today has told me he is having more fun now than when he started working in the NFL. In life today, if you're not having fun, you'd better get away from the job. Life is too short. I don't even watch games anymore. I watch the summaries and highlights.

Year-Round Officials

Some people have raised the point about having the NFL officials paid on an annual basis and their full-time job would be working for the league. I just don't see this working. The issue came up in the early 1980s. When Art McNally ran a survey he found that he would lose 60 percent of his officials. Too many officials were already successful in their chosen professions and while willing to give up 20 weekends a year, plus time for special clinics, would not make a commitment 7 days a week, 12 months a year. For me, that would really kill any fun in being an NFL official.

Invariably, the people who said they would stay on year-round were the ones just coming into the league or the veterans getting ready to retire from their other jobs. We would have wiped out the guts of our staff.–Art McNally

Another question that faced the league was what would you do with the officials from Monday through Saturday? One suggestion was to have the officials work with the teams by assigning three to four to a team, beginning with training camp. The crew would watch practice and act as an official to make calls during scrimmages. Many teams don't scrimmage during the season the way they used to. There is too great a chance of injury to a key player. The workouts are not like they are in pre-season. I didn't see this working out either.

It isn't the same kind of pressure during practice as there is during a game. There is no television and perhaps 500 to 1,000 fans in the stands. Not like game day at all. The moment of truth is when everything counts and every call is being scrutinized by millions of people. Having officials year-round would not improve efficiency any appreciable amount.–Art McNally

Having officials full-time, year-round in the NFL will be hard to do. However, it might be the best way to go with the game getting so big now. We get the quality of official now because people have other jobs. The league will never pay enough to get the best full time.–Mike Ditka

The Best Crew for the Super Bowl?

During the playoffs each year, and especially during the Super Bowl, we always hear people wanting to change the way the officials are selected. Now it is done on a grading system and as individuals, not by teams. Crews could be ranked numerically. Those with all veterans would probably rank the highest. An outstanding crew with a rookie and one or more younger officials, might not rank the highest even though the team's referee or umpire or side judge might be ranked #1 for the season. It takes five years for a good official to be an NFL official. Those in their second and third years could keep one of the very best from working post-season games.

> The veterans who are selected to officiate the Super Bowl know the mechanics of the game so well that you could take their numbers off and move them to different positions and they would work very well together as a crew because they all know where they must be on every play. I know how John Madden feels, and have for years, about having the best team of officials be on the field to officiate the Super Bowl game between the best two teams. There is always the chance that one of the seven officials could be a rookie. And the rookie is the one most vulnerable to making a mistake.–
> Art McNally

I wonder how television analyst Madden would explain to his viewers an error made by a rookie when the best official at that position is home watching the game. By selecting crews, I believe it puts too much pressure on those with minimal league experience to be under pressure of having to be perfect for the most important game of the season. Mistakes will happen and most likely it will be a judgment call. This is where years of experience being under fire make it critical for a veteran to be on the field.

My All-Time Team

The greatest football official that I have ever worked with and seen in my 35 years of experience, including the 27 I worked in the NFL, was Jerry Bergman. He would be my headlinesman. He was the finest rules official, the gutsiest on the field official, extremely loyal and a great friend. He had to overcome great physical adversity as a young man to become a great athlete himself and then went on to be the best of the best, in my opinion. He and I traveled together for six years. We had a philosophy that said "If you can't have fun, and be the best there is, then don't do it." This philosophy, of course, goes against the grain of the philosophy of the league office the way it was when we both were in the league and the way it is today.

My choice for umpire would be the late Tom Hensley, who worked nine seasons with me. As I did with Jerry Bergman, Tom and I became the closest of friends. He was dependable, tough and had a great understanding of the game. He was a former Golden Gloves boxing champion and was a starting lineman at Tennessee under General Neyland.

My selection for line judge will be a surprise to most officials. I worked with many great line judges. Since these are my personal picks, they are the people I would feel most comfortable going into battle with. I would want Wilson Gosier to be my line judge. He was with me five years and came into the league as an outstanding deep back college official. The league office was very critical of Wilson and ready to let him go at the end of the season. When I was told there was no way to save him, I gave it my best shot.

During the last half of the season, Wilson became a tremendous NFL football official and to this day should be in the NFL. He was never given a fair chance to learn the game as an NFL official. It was the league's loss because the end of his last season he was terrific. I called McNally following the Super Bowl to suggest it would be a mistake to let Wilson go. Art listened to what I said. However, he thought I was calling only because Wilson asked me to intervene in his behalf. Wilson never asked me for help at all. Art found this out later. Being unwilling to change, cost the NFL a potentially great official. The following season, Ralph Morcroft, one of the all-time great umpires, told me he had seen someone he considered one of the best of college officials. It was Wilson Gosier, doing what he does best, working at a deep position.

My choice for the three deep positions would be any of five men: Dick Hantack, Vince Jacobs, Donnie Orr, Dean Look and Bob Wortman. Dick Hantack is now one of the finest referees in the league, if not the finest. The first playoff game I ever worked was with Vince Jacobs. I had tremendous faith in him and told him to take everything that was deep as his assignment for the game. Vince had a heart attack during the season and passed away.

Donnie, a quarterback at Vanderbilt, worked with me for 14 seasons, longer than anyone else. Dean was a quarterback at Michigan State and played one season at third base for the Chicago White Sox. He had a great talent for the game as did all of the others. His great sense of humor was important to me and the entire crew as he did his job and was both amusing and entertaining. Bob Wortman, the final deep official on my all-star team, said the reason Vince had a heart attack was because of the way I ran our officiating crew. Of course he was joking.

My pick for the official that I enjoyed most during his rookie year was Bill Carrollo who also has moved up to be a referee. He has a great business background and is with IBM. He is gutsy, had a great sense of humor and was able to do a super job in his first year.

Why did I enjoy these people more than any of the others I worked with in my 27 years in the league? We always seemed to be on the same wave length. Each person had an independence about him and a defiance of the status quo, being willing to step up and make the great call at the toughest time. They were never intimidated by the league office or any of their supervisors.

If it sounds like my team is a guerrilla outfit, working outside the system of rigid control of the league office mandate "Do it this way or you're gone," then you're probably right. When Jerry Bergman and I came into the league we were interviewed by the former supervisor of officials, Mark Duncan, a former San Francisco 49er coach who later went to Seattle to become head of player personnel. I was fortunate also to have support from Dan Rooney of the Steelers.

Berggie and I always said that in the 27 years we were in the league together, prior to my retirement, that Mark never called either of us by our first names. The last time we saw him, I was a referee and Jerry a head linesman and we had a pre-season night game in Seattle. We had two rookies on our team with us. Mark stopped by our dressing room to say hello and visited with all of the other five officials, calling them by their first name. He then waved to Berggie and me and said, "How's it going." We always enjoyed our status as far as he was concerned. No one from the league office were participatory managers. They were all authoritarian, control freaks.

Unfortunately, it has only gotten worse. I don't believe this would have ever happened if Pete Rozelle were still the commissioner. Paul Tagliabue is a lawyer.

APPENDIX A

Biography of Frederick Mount Wyant

Father, grandfather, poet, author, businessman, motivational-speaker, athlete and official, Fred Wyant was born April 26, 1934 in Weston, W. Va. He was a three-sport star in football, baseball and basketball for Weston High School. Then 5'11" and 205 pounds with a 17" neck, he went on to become one of the greatest quarterbacks in West Virginia University history, where he majored in chemical engineering. He is the only quarterback to lead the Mountaineers and its T-formation, option play offense to three straight wins against Penn State (1953, 1954 and 1955). As a starter he compiled a regular season record of 30 wins and only 4 losses and guided WVU to the Sugar Bowl on January 1, 1954. He is the winningest quarterback in Mountaineer history.

He has written 11 books on happiness in parenting and traveled the country giving lectures on that subject and as a motivational speaker. He was named a "Famous Poet for 1996" and a "Diamond Homer Recipient" by the Famous Poets Society.

There was no such thing as two-platoon football in the early and mid-50s and Wyant was defensive safety when he wasn't playing quarterback. In many games he played the full 60 minutes.

A left-handed passer and considered a dangerous runner, he still ranks among the WVU career top 10 in total offense (3,426 yards), passing yardage (2,663), pass attempts (401) and touchdown passes

(21). His 83-yard touchdown pass to Harry Sweeney against Fordham in 1954 is still the fourth longest in the school's history. He accounted for 708 plays in his career and was responsible for 41 touchdowns.

Wyant got his break as a freshman when underdog Furman was beating heavily favored WVU 22-0 going into the fourth quarter. He promptly led the team to two quick touchdowns and was driving for the third and winning score when time ran out.

He gained national recognition in 1952 when he led the Mountaineers to a 16-0 win over Pitt after the Panthers had beaten Notre Dame and Army on previous weekends.

One of his greatest games was the 1954 season opening win against nationally-ranked South Carolina in Columbia. The convincing 26-6 win over the Gamecocks after their victory over highly ranked Army propelled the Mountaineers into the national rankings.

Stonewall Jackson lived near Wyant's hometown of Weston. Someone wrote in *The Weston Democrat* that "Wyant was the greatest field general since Stonewall Jackson." During his years at WVU, the team had its pre-season training camp at nearby Jackson's Mill.

WVU Football Records:

1952 Won 7 Lost 2
1953 Won 8 Lost 2
1954 Won 8 Lost 1
1955 Won 8 Lost 2

Honors:

1952

College Football's Freshman of the Year, NEA Service
All-Southern Conference, second-team, Southern Conference Sports
    Writers
All-Chemical All-American

1953

All-East, *Collier's Magazine*
Sophomore Back of the Year, *Saturday Evening Post*
All-Southern Conference by Southern Conference Sports Writers, United
Press and Associated Press
Academic All-American, third team
All-Chemical All-American

1954

All-Southern Conference, Southern Conference Sports Writers, Associated Press and United Press
Southern Conference Player of the Year
All-Chemical All-American
Academic All-American, first team
All-Southern Conference, Scholastic All-Conference, American Peoples
Encyclopedia Co.
All-South, *New York Daily News*
All-American, honorable mention, Associated Press, NEA Service, United
Press and International News Service (Note: Wyant received more
All-American nomination votes for Associated Press than any other
player from the Southern Conference)

1955

All-Southern Conference, Southern Conference Sports Writers and
Associated Press
All-Chemical All-American
He starred in the North-South Shrine All-Star game in Miami in December 1955.

He completed a 95-yard touchdown pass and led a team of college all-stars against a team of professional all-stars in the Hula Bowl All-Star game in Honolulu in January 1956. He led the college team to three touchdowns in the second half.

Academic All-American, second team, by Les Jordan

All-Southern Conference, Scholastic All-Conference, American Peoples Encyclopedia Co.

All-American, honorable mention, *Collier's Magazine*, Associated Press and United Press

Quotes:

Many football men rate Freddy Wyant of West Virginia the best college split-T quarterback in the country.–Arch Ward, *Chicago Tribune*

Freddy Wyant has so much driving power on the option play he runs like most college fullbacks.–Shelley Rolfe, *Richmond Times-Dispatch*

He's the best I've seen on the option play.–Art Lewis, Wyant's head football coach at WVU

Cool and poised and slick as a damn bandit . . . a bull.–Chauncey Durden, *Richmond Times-Dispatch*

He was considered a major league baseball prospect and during the 1954 season he started at first base and hit .407. He played in industrial leagues during the summer months and consistently batted around the .450 mark.

Washington Redskins–1956

Wyant was the third round draft choice for the Redskins. He was the starting quarterback in the opening pre-season exhibition game in the Piedmont Bowl and went head-to-head with Green Bay's Bart Starr. He completed 10 of 14 passes for 181 yards and two touchdowns to lead Washington to a victory. He started the next two pre-season games before seriously injuring his ankle which kept him out of action until late in the season. During the season he played behind Eddie LeBaron as the stand-by quarterback.

The Redskins' media guide says "Because of his speed and sure tackling, Wyant also was used on the Suicide Squad." In one game as quarterback against the St. Louis Cardinals, he completed one pass in two attempts for a 17-yard gain.

Toronto Argonauts–1957

He played in 8 games as Toronto, under coach Hampton Pool, compiled a record of 4 wins and 10 losses. Wyant rushed 10 times for 23 yards and 2 touchdowns and scored a total of 12 points. He attempted 72 passes and completed 28 for 440 yards with 8 interceptions. The average gain per pass was 6.11 yards and his longest pass was 43 yards.

NFL

Fred Wyant began his NFL career as a line judge during the 1966 season. He was in this position for five years through the 1970 season. For 19 years, from 1971 through the 1989 season he was a referee. In 1990 he returned to the line judge position for three years before retiring at the end of the 1992 season.

Following were his playoff games, all as a referee:

AFC-NFC Pro Bowl, Monday, January 23, 1978, Tampa, Florida

NFC 14, AFC 13

Walter Payton, the NFL's leading rusher in 1977, sparked a second-half comeback to give the NFC a one-point win and tie the series between the two conferences at four victories each. Payton, who was the game's Most Valuable Player, gained 77 yards on 13 carries.

AFC	3	10	0	0–13
NFC	0	0	7	7–14

> AFC–FG, Toni Linhart, 21
> AFC–Clifford Branch, 10 pass from Ken Stabler (Linhart kick)
> AFC–FG, Linhart, 39
> NFC–Terry Metcalf, 4 pass from Pat Haden, (Efren Herrera kick)
> NFC–Walter Payton, 1 run (Herrera kick)

1981 AFC Divisional Playoff, January 2, 1982, Miami, Florida

San Diego Chargers 41, Miami Dolphins 38
(Overtime)

This game was a record-setting showcase of the passing game and ended with the most points scored in an NFL playoff (79), the most total yards (1,036), the only game in NFL history in which two quarterbacks passed for more than 400 yards and the most dramatic as San Diego outlasted Miami in overtime.

The Chargers jumped off to a 24-0 lead in the first quarter but Miami came back with 17 unanswered points in the second quarter to make it a 24-17 game at halftime. The game was tied 31-31 at the end of three periods.

Miami quarterback Don Strock completed 29 of 43 passes for 403 yards and four touchdowns but Chargers' quarterback Dan Fouts, who passed for an NFL-record 4,802 yards during the regular season, completed 33 of 43 passes for 433 yards.

As the game went into overtime, San Diego won the toss, received and drove from its own 13 to the Miami 8. On second-and-goal at 9:15, Rolf Benirschke's 27-yard field goal attempt was wide to the left. Miami and San Diego each had two possessions before the Dolphins got the ball the third time. Miami drove from the San Diego 46 down to the 17 yard line. On fourth-and-two at 11:27, Uwe von Schamann attempted a 34-yard field goal that was blocked by Kellen Winslow, who also caught 13 passes. Chargers quarterback Dan Fouts connected on four of five passes, including a 38-yard completion to Charley Joiner, and moved the ball 74 yards in six plays to get the ball on the Miami 10. On first down, Benirschke kicked a 29-yard field goal for the Chargers win after 13:52 of overtime play.

The following week Cincinnati beat the Chargers 27-7 in the AFC championship game, but lost to the San Francisco 49ers 26-21 in Super bowl XVI in Pontiac, Michigan.

San Diego	24	0	7	7	3–41
Miami	0	17	14	7	0–38

San Diego–FG, Rolf Benirschke, 32

San Diego–Chandler, 58 punt return (Benirschke kick)

San Diego–Chuck Muncie, 1 run (Benirschke kick)

San Diego–Brooks, 8 pass from Dan Fouts (Benirschke kick)

Miami–FG, Uwe von Schamann, 34

Miami–Rose, 1 pass from Don Strock (von Schamann kick)

Miami–Nathan, 40 pass play; Harris, 15 pass from Strock, Nathan, 25 lateral from Harris (von Schamann kick)

Miami-Rose, 15 pass from Strock (von Schamann kick)

San Diego–Kellen Winslow, 25 pass from Fouts (Benirschke kick)

Miami–Hardy, 50 pass from Strock (von Schamann kick)

Miami–12, run (von Schamann kick)

San Diego–Brooks, 9 pass from Fouts (Benirschke kick)

San Diego–FG, Benirschke, 29

1982 NFC Divisional Playoff, January 8, 1983, Green Bay, Wisconsin

Green Bay Packers 41, St. Louis Cardinals 16

Quarterback Lynn Dickey, who still holds the Packers individual record for passing yards in a single season, threw four touchdown passes to lead Green Bay to its playoff win. He completed 17 of 23 passes for 260 yards. Statistically the Cardinals outplayed the Packers in every category but the final score.

In the next round, Dallas defeated Green Bay 37-26 in Dallas, but lost to Washington 31-17 for the NFC championship. The Redskins went on to beat Miami 27-17 in Super Bowl XVII played at the Rose Bowl in Pasadena.

Green Bay	7	21	10	3–41
St. Louis	3	6	0	7–16

St. Louis–FG, O'Donoghue, 18

Green Bay–Jefferson, pass from Dickey, 50 (Stenerud kick)

Green Bay–Lofton, pass from Dickey, 20 (Stenerud kick)

Green Bay–Ivery, 2 run (Stenerud kick)

Green Bay–Ivery, pass from Dickey, 4 (Stenerud kick)

St. Louis–Tilley, pass from Lomax, 5 (O'Donoghue kick blocked by Lewis)

Green Bay–FG, Stenerud 46

Green Bay–Jefferson, pass from Dickey, 7 (Stenerud kick)

Green Bay–FG, Stenerud, 34

St. Louis–Schumann, pass from Lomax, 18 (O'Donoghue kick)

ENR

1983 AFC Divisional Playoff, December 31, 1983, Miami, Florida

Seattle 27, Miami 20

The dolphins saw their season end on a sour note as they lost to Seattle in the semi-final round of the AFC playoff at the Orange Bowl. It was the first time in the playoffs for the Seahawks in their eight-year history. Miami rookie quarterback Dan Marino returned from a December 4th knee injury and got the Dolphins on the scoreboard first and to a 13-6 halftime lead with two touchdown passes. With only 3:43 left, Miami's Gerald Small ran back an intercepted pass to the Seattle 2 where Woody Bennett ran it in to give the Dolphins a 20-17 lead. Dave Kreig connected twice with Steve Largent for 56 yards to put Seattle ahead 24-20. Miami's Fulton Walker fumbled the Seattle kickoff which led to a 37-yard field goal by Norm Johnson. Another Walker fumble on the next kickoff iced the game for Seattle.

Seattle lost to Oakland 30-14 in the AFC championship game. The Raiders went on to win Super Bowl XVIII in Tampa beating the defending champion Washington Redskins 38-9.

| Seattle | 0 | 7 | 7 | 13–27 |
| Miami | 0 | 13 | 0 | 7–20 |

Miami–Dan Johnson, 19 pass from Dan Marino (von Schamann kick failed)

Seattle–Cullen Bryant, 6 pass from Dave Kreig (Norm Johnson kick)

Miami–Mark Duper, 32 pass from Marino (von Schamann kick)

Seattle–Curt Warner, 1 run (Johnson kick)

Seattle–FG, Johnson, 27

Miami–Woody Bennett, 2 run (von Schamann kick)

Seattle–Warner, 2 run (Johnson kick)

Seattle–FG, Johnson, 37

1984 AFC Divisional Playoff, December 30, 1984, Denver, Colorado

Pittsburgh 24, Denver 17

Denver had two possessions in the final two minutes of the game and couldn't score as the Steelers advanced to the AFC championship game. The Broncos recovered two Pittsburgh fumbles in the first quarter. Rich Karlis' field goal attempt was wide on the first recovery but the Steelers fumbled on the very next play and this time John Elway connected on a seven-yard pass to Jim Wright for a touchdown. Pittsburgh went ahead 10-7 at halftime, and broke away from a 17-17 tie when Erick Williams intercepted an Elway pass and returned it to the Denver 2 with only 2:45 left in the game. Two plays later, Frank Pollard ran it in for the score.

The Steelers lost the conference championship 45-28 to Miami. The Dolphins lost Super Bowl XIX to San Francisco 38-16 at Stanford.

Pittsburgh	0	10	7	7–24
Denver	7	0	10	0–17

    Denver–Jim Wright, 9 pass from John Elway (Rich Karlis kick)
    Pittsburgh–FG, Gary Anderson, 28
    Pittsburgh–Frank Pollard, 1 run (Anderson kick)
    Denver–FG, Karlis, 21
    Denver–Steve Watson, 20 pass from Elway (Karlis kick)
    Pittsburgh–Louis Lipps, 10 pass from Mark Malone (Anderson kick)
    Pittsburgh–Pollard, 2 run (Anderson kick)

APPENDIX B

Famous Poet for 1996

Congratulations!

Fred Wyant

Diamond Homer Recipient

The Executive committee of the Famous Poets Society deemed this poem worthy of a formal presentation during their Second Annual Poetry Convention in Anaheim, California, on September 27, 1996.

TODAY

Today you appeared as a flower in the Spring
With a smile and radiance of a Heavenly Being
A blanket of Black Velvet, a field of White snow
A sweetness of life that only God could know
The sun shone around you, the wind gently blew
My heart stopped a second and everyone knew
The mold had been set, here was my life
A softness, a beauty, a lover, a wife?
Would this moment escape me, could it fade like the day?
Will another one like you someday pass my way
A freshness, a tenderness, the Spell has been cast
My wish forever had happened at last
Though yet I can't touch you, though yet we're apart
Someday in the future, you'll be in my heart

I love you, I knew it, It won't disappear
If God will forgive me, be near my Dear

FMW

Famous Poets Society, Hollywood, California

APPENDIX C

Biography of Rene A. Henry

Rene A. Henry, Fellow PRSA, has had diverse careers in public relations, sports marketing and management, housing and construction, television and entertainment, politics, higher education and as a trade association CEO.

In the mid-70s, he co-founded ICPR which became the second largest international public relations firm in the West with headquarters in Los Angeles and offices in New York, Washington and Paris. It was the first public relations or advertising agency in the U.S. to establish Hispanic Marketing and Sports Marketing Divisions. He has counseled *Fortune 500* companies, leaders in entertainment, sports, and politics, and even foreign governments, on a myriad of issues and crises.

Henry also was president and CEO of the National Institute of Building Sciences, Washington, D.C.; worked with Mayor Tom Bradley and his team to direct international media activities to help Los Angeles get the 1984 Olympic Games; and was a senior member of George Bush's 1988 presidential campaign staff. He later served in the Bush Administration and was a member of the team at the U.S. Department of Labor that researched and wrote *The Glass Ceiling Initiative.*

From 1991-1996 he was executive director of university relations and on the president's executive cabinet at Texas A&M University in College Station. In 1996 he joined the U.S. Environmental Protection Agency as director of the Office of Communications & Government

Relations for the mid-Atlantic states region based in Philadelphia. He also has advised the Chilean government on manufactured housing and how to create a secondary mortgage market.

He has created and produced award-winning videos and television documentaries and authored books on land investment, utility cogeneration, sports and public relations. He authored the definitive book on crisis communications, *You'd Better Have a Hose If You Want to Put Out the Fire*, which was published in January 2000. His *Marketing Public Relations–the hows that make it work!* is used by professionals, professors and students and was republished in paperback in February 2000. *Offsides!* is his sixth book. His first book, *How to Profitably Buy and Sell Land*, was one of the best selling on the subject. He co-authored two other books–*Bears Handbook–stories, stats and stuff about Baylor University Football* and *MIUS and You–the developer looks at a new utility concept*.

His honors include three *Silver Anvils* from the Public Relations Society of America, two CINE *Golden Eagles*, three Creative Excellence in Black Advertising awards, the *Clarion Award for Human Rights* from Women In Communications, *Distinguished Citizen Award* from the PRSA Los Angeles chapter, "Best In Texas" *Silver Spurs*, a silver and two bronze medals from WorldFest Houston International Film Festival and numerous awards and citations from professional organizations for campaigns and excellence in public relations.

He is a member of the Academy of Motion Picture Arts & Sciences and the Academy of Television Arts & Sciences. He has judged the Primetime Emmy awards 10 times as well as international film and TV festivals in Italy and Hungary. In 2001 he served as chair of the College of Fellows of the Public Relations Society of America and served on the executive board of the PRSA Environmental Section and on the board of directors of the Philadelphia PRSA chapter.

He received his A.B. degree in economics from The College of William & Mary, did graduate study in marketing at West Virginia University and has taken executive courses at Harvard University.

Printed in the United States
3283